Émile Théodore Joseph Hubert Banning

Africa and the Brussels Geographical Conference

Émile Théodore Joseph Hubert Banning

Africa and the Brussels Geographical Conference

ISBN/EAN: 9783337349318

Printed in Europe, USA, Canada, Australia, Japan

Cover: Foto ©Suzi / pixelio.de

More available books at **www.hansebooks.com**

AND THE

BRUSSELS GEOGRAPHICAL CONFERENCE.

BY

EMILE BANNING,
MEMBER OF THE CONFERENCE.

TRANSLATED BY

RICHARD HENRY MAJOR, F.S.A.

WITH A MAP.

LONDON:
SAMPSON LOW, MARSTON, SEARLE & RIVINGTON,
CROWN BUILDINGS, 188 FLEET STREET.
1877.

All rights reserved.

LONDON:
PRINTED BY WILLIAM CLOWES AND SONS,
STAMFORD STREET AND CHARING CROSS.

MEMORANDUM BY THE TRANSLATOR.

In placing in the hands of the English reader the following highly interesting summary of African geography, I wish to say that I hold myself responsible for no expression or omission therein, beyond such as the critic may find liable to censure in the translation itself. The text has not been interfered with, except in the conversion of mètres into feet, and kilomètres into miles.

R. H. MAJOR.

PREFACE.

THE object of the Author in publishing this work has been to promote, as far as lay in his power, an undertaking which will hereafter do honour to the intelligence of the present century, and which, in his opinion, is pregnant with benefits to the various branches of the human family, whether the most advanced in the paths of civilisation, or the most behind-hand. The special duty which he had to perform at the Conference which gave birth to this undertaking, placed it in his power to gain, perhaps, the most intimate insight into its object and tendencies, and to determine, with some degree of certainty, the scope of its movements. Nevertheless, he feels it necessary to state that, in acquitting himself of this task, he has only consulted, and given expression to, his own personal convictions. The considerations offered, and the opinions uttered, throw no responsibility on any but himself, and in claiming them entirely for his own he is but fulfilling a duty.

BRUSSELS,
November 10, 1876.

INTRODUCTION.

TOWARDS the middle of the month of September, 1876, there was brought together in the palace at Brussels, under the presidency of, and in virtue of the initiative taken by, the King of the Belgians, an International Conference, summoned for the purpose of bringing about a solution of one of the greatest problems which have perplexed science and philanthropy in these latter times. From the nature of its object, as well as from the exceptional character of its composition, this assembly could not fail of awakening interest, both at home and abroad. Whatever may be the engrossing subjects of anxiety of the present hour, it was a great and noble thought to induce men's minds to lay them aside for a moment, and to concentrate their attention upon one of general and paramount interest to the human race. When from the mountain peaks of history we take a survey of the world's surface, many unanticipated rays of brightness light up the horizon of nations, and reveal fresh fields for their activity. While the old nations of Europe, not content with their limited boundaries, are constantly increasing the circle of their efforts in the cause of civilisation, it is impossible to avoid forecasting in our minds what are the approaching destinies of a vast continent, three times the size of Europe, with a population of two hundred millions, and, one might say, touching, with its northern seaboard, Spain, Sicily, and Greece. Four centuries have sufficed for covering both the Americas with civilised and prosperous states. India has become an English province, and Central Asia is becoming a Russian province; Japan is assuming the aspect of an European state; China, by force of circumstances, is becoming open to the influences of diplomacy and commerce, while Australia and New Zealand are reproducing at the Antipodes some of the political and social institutions of England.

All the time that this wonderful conquest has been going on, Africa has remained buried in its solitude, stretched out, like a gigantic Helot, at the feet of apathetic Europe. No effort, of any moment, at colonisation or propagandism, has been made since the sixteenth century to penetrate the secrets of its physical or social condition, or to draw it into that broad and powerful current which is tending to unite more and more in one common effort all the dispersed races of the world. The present generation has in its youth seen the map of Central Africa as empty and as bare as that of the Pole. This fate of a continent which has seen arise on its soil the most ancient civilisation of the world, and which in its day imposed its influence on Asia and Europe, will remain hereafter a riddle in history. For four hundred years after the days of Bartholomew Diaz and Vasco da Gama, the geographical conformation of the African Continent, and the history and habits of its populations, lay buried in profound darkness. On the seaboard, the nations of Europe had established scarcely any connections with the natives, beyond such as arose out of the abominable practice of the slave trade; and, on the north, the Sahara seemed an impassable barrier, which condemned to eternal isolation and inferiority the races which it protected even by its dangers and its terrors.

A new era has at length commenced for this land of slavery and mystery. The thick veil with which ignorance and prejudice had enveloped Africa is being torn in every direction. Fearless travellers, brave missionaries, have, for five and twenty years past, penetrated it from north to south, from east to west. Many a halting-place is dotted with tombs; but devotion to science and humanity is confronting and surmounting all obstacles. Every year adds a province to our knowledge, and deep openings are being made in every direction in the interior of the African Continent.

It is this nucleus of Central Africa, a vast region which extends, on both sides of the equator, over a surface of nearly 2,400,000 square miles,* which remains to be explored. Its limits are traced by the expeditions of Barth, of Rohlfs, of Nachtigal on the

---

* The empire of Germany measures 324,377 square miles; France, 317,146. It is, therefore, more than seven times as large as either of these two countries.

north; of Schweinfurth, Baker, Gordon, and Stanley on the east; of Livingstone and Cameron on the south; of Tuckey and Du Chaillu, of Güssfeldt, of Marche and Compiègne on the west. It is with the view of solving this last problem, of easing the labour which it imposes, and, if possible, of diminishing its dangers, by the combination of individual and national efforts, that Leopold II. has convoked the Conference at Brussels. If this generous initiative, which in itself is a weighty fact, should meet with the sympathy of public opinion, it is clear that science will not stand alone in reaping the benefits. A virgin and fruitful soil, and numerous races of men, for the most part better endowed than is commonly supposed, will be rescued from an isolation of centuries; the task of civilising Africa, hitherto conducted with insufficient means, will acquire a broad and stable basis. The slave trade, that scourge of the African races, may be reached and grappled with at its source. Who could calculate, from this moment, what may be the influences on the social and economical conditions of Europe and Asia produced by regular and continuous relations with an entirely new branch of the human family?

The indication of these points exhibits the extent of the idea which has prevailed at the Conference of Brussels, and the scope of its undertaking. Such great results, however, will not be obtained without sustained effort and serious sacrifices. The co-operation of all is necessary to the success of the crusade which is intended to be undertaken, and that co-operation will not be active, devoted, or persistent, unless its object is perfectly understood. Have the expeditions for discovery in Africa during this century assumed a special character? What system or what bond has there been in them? Have they led to decisive results? What is the present state of our knowledge of Africa? What do we know of the general aspect of its soil, of the elevations of its surface, of the distribution of its waters? What are its climate and resources? To what families do the races which inhabit it belong? To what degree of civilisation have they raised themselves? Do there exist reasons for believing that they may reach higher? What is the slave trade of the nineteenth century? How and by whom is it carried on?

Here are so many questions to which it seems desirable that at least the principles of a solution should be indicated, and the more so that, through a regretable and unique exception, there has hitherto existed in Belgium no Geographical Society taking upon itself the charge of agitating and incessantly discussing under the public eye these grave and important problems. The making common a collection of succinct but well reasoned-out ideas on all these objects will enable the undertaking of the Congress to assume the double character indispensable to its success: viz.—a course of action, both scientific and civilising, directed by the highest influences, and at the same time supported by all the resources of popular sympathy.

FIRST PART.

AFRICA:

VIEWED HISTORICALLY, PHYSICALLY, AND SOCIALLY.

FIRST PART.

AFRICA:

VIEWED HISTORICALLY, PHYSICALLY, AND SOCIALLY.

CHAPTER I.

HISTORICAL SKETCH OF DISCOVERIES IN AFRICA IN THE 19TH CENTURY.

THE movement in the direction of geographical discovery in Africa, which, since 1840, has been carried on with admirable energy and perseverance, is one of the most interesting spectacles of the present century: a century which has been in other respects fruitful in great scientific enterprises. It might be said that in giving so remarkable an extension and activity to this movement, the nations of Europe had, by tacit consent, been influenced by one thought: viz., that of opening up to the exertions, and admitting to the conquests of civilisation, a continent, which, without any reasonable explanation, had become the object of systematic abandonment. For a long period it had seemed that Africa was doomed to go back rather than advance in this direction. Egypt, which, in the beginning of history, held so high a rank in the world, and propagated towards the south its institutions and customs to distances scarcely now recognisable, seemed to have outlived her mission. The rich and industrious populations which antiquity saw established on the shores of the Mediterranean, at Carthage, in Cyrenaica, Numidia, and Mauritania, had disappeared, leaving scarcely any traces of their passage. Barbarism had again taken possession of those beautiful provinces which the Roman dominion had brought to so high a pitch of cultivation. In the middle ages, Islamism swept like a torrent over Northern Africa from one end to the other, but though it deeply modified the condition of men's minds, and raised up ideas and habits which have resisted the effect of time, it has nowhere founded any important or durable political establishment.

We must come down to the fifteenth century to get a glimpse of the dawn of a new era. Till then, a very imperfect idea was formed of the configuration of Africa, and, from Ptolemy's time downwards, scientific notions respecting it were rather away from, than near to, the truth. They had no sort of a correct idea of any but the northern region, and even the ancient maps of Sanudo, of Bianco and of Fra Mauro outrageously distorted its outlines. The maritime expeditions of the Portuguese, the origination of, and perseverance in, which have immortalised the name of one of their greatest princes, Henry the Navigator, revealed a new world. In 1434, Cape Bojador was rounded; in 1482, the Gulf of Guinea was explored; in 1487, Bartholomew Diaz reached and even passed the Cape of Good Hope, and before the close of the century, from 1497 to 1499, Vasco da Gama doubled the promontory, and sailed along the eastern coast as far as Arabia. The map of Diego Ribera, published in 1529, in Seville, and that of Dapper, which appeared in 1676 at Amsterdam, gave for the first time the exact profile of the African Continent; this latter seems even to have out-stepped in many respects the progress of modern geography.

Numerous commercial establishments were founded soon after on the coasts of Africa, and efforts at colonisation were made, but nevertheless they did not go beyond the sea coast, taking very little extension into the interior. The Portuguese, in fact, early explored a great part of Central Africa, and forestalled on the banks of the Zambesi, as well as in the basin of the Congo, some of Livingstone's grand discoveries. After them, the French, in Senegambia, and the Dutch, at the Cape of Good Hope, penetrated the vast continent of Africa, but without considerably adding to the results to science effected by the efforts of the Portuguese. The interior of that immense plateau, the first stages of which show themselves at a few leagues' distance from the sea, remained covered with an impenetrable mystery.

With the foundation in 1788 of the celebrated African Association of London, commenced that great movement of exploration, which in our days only has taken its complete extension. Expeditions were multiplied; they were organised on a constructive plan, and assumed a scientific character. Africa was attacked at three points at one time. At the close of the eighteenth century, expeditions started from Tripoli on the north, from Nubia on the east, and from the Gambia on the west. The German, Hornemann, and, above all, the Scotchman, Mungo Park, were the heroes and also the first victims of these enterprises.

In the Gulf of Guinea debouches a river, which, by its enormous development, the complication of its course, and the mystery of its source, presents striking analogies with the Nile: this is the Niger. From an early time the exertions of travellers were directed to the solution of this hydrographic problem. In the beginning of this century, Mungo Park penetrated by the Gambia into the basin of the Niger. Exposed to unceasing attacks from the natives, and suffering the severest hardships, he, nevertheless, descended the course of the river as far as Bussa, where he died, after having seen most of his travelling companions perish before him. Nevertheless, this expedition did not fail to call forth numerous successors. In 1818, a French traveller, Mollien, reattempted the enterprise of Mungo Park: he did not reach the Niger, but he determined the sources of the Senegal, the Gambia, and the Rio Grande. After him, two Englishmen, Lander and Laird, explored the mouths of the great river, which the former descended from Bussa (1830 to 1832). Baikie, whose remarkable expedition took place in 1854, starting from the coast of Guinea, reached as far as the junction of the Benué, an imposing river, which he ascended as far as Iola, the extreme point attained by Barth in descending from the north. Some years later, at the instance of General Faidherbe, then Governor of Senegambia, several officers of the French marine, Lambert (1860), Mage and Quintin (1863-66), examined the upper course of the Niger. In 1869, Winwood Reade approached the sources in those mountains near the sea, which form the eastern boundary of the settlement of Sierra Leone. In spite of the gaps which have still to be filled up, it was an important conquest over inner Africa; the basin of the Niger, in fact, incloses a host of populous tribes, and of states having at least a beginning of organisation. The recent expedition of the English against Ashanti has, for its part, shed new light on regions, in the neighbourhood, of surprising fertility, which, as yet, present no obstacles to the efforts of civilisation, beyond the heat of a torrid climate and the deadly miasma of its swamps.

On the north and west, Algeria and Senegal have become, in the hands of the French, points of attack in the direction of the great desert of Sahara, which reaches the boundaries of their possessions. In this direction they at once encounter the most inhospitable part of it, the Sahel, a vast sandy arid plain, dotted with a few rare oases, and inhabited at different points by tribes justly dreaded for their cruelty. It was a French traveller, Caillié, who, starting from the Senegal, first visited, in 1828, the mysterious city of Timbuctoo on the Niger, on the southern borders of the Sahara. After him, Leop. Panet travelled along its western border from St. Louis to Mogadore by Aderer (1852). More recently still, in 1859, one of the most learned geographers of our time, H. Duveyrier, explored with exceptional success that sea of sand in which so many dauntless travellers have perished. There, in especial, died in 1869, murdered by her escort, a woman whose great and numerous travels in Africa have made her famous, Alexine Tinné of the Hague. Further eastwards, the Sahara changes its aspect; the soil becomes stony; the oases increase in number, and the population is less sparse, until we reach the immediate vicinity of Egypt, where the desert resumes its sway. In the winter of 1873-74, Gerhard Rohlfs, who had already at this time won renown by considerable enterprises at the most opposite points of northern Africa, led an expedition into this latter region, known as the Libyan Desert, the remarkable results of which he has lately published.

South of this region, and at several points interblending with it, is the Soudan, which has lately been the object of noteworthy attempts. This is the heart of Africa; here commences the country of that negro race which is scattered, southwards, over the whole extent of the great African plateau. England and Germany have contributed the most in late years to increase our knowledge of these previously almost entirely unknown countries. In 1823, Clapperton discovered Lake Chad, the great inland basin which receives the waters of the vast hollow of which the central plateau and that of the Sahara form the borders. It is on the confines of this lake that are grouped the most advanced and populous states of the Soudan, specially those of Bornou, of Kanem, of Bagirmi and of Wadai. The latter borders on Darfur, which has just passed into the sovereignty of Egypt.

In 1849 took place the great expedition of Richardson, Overweg, and Barth, of whom the last only returned and published in 1855 the touching narrative of the journey. Starting from Tripoli, the expedition had crossed the Sahara by a new route, penetrated into the Soudan, and reached Lake Chad. After the death of his companions, Barth turned his steps westwards as far as the Niger, and visited Timbuctoo, which no European, since him, has seen. Vogel, proceeding on his tracks, arrived in 1856 in the Wadai, but there he was assassinated by order of the sultan of that state. Seven expeditions in succession went in search of him. One of them, led by Beurmann, reached the goal, but likewise at the cost of the life of its leader (1863).

From 1865 to 1867 Gerhard Rohlfs, who had previously attracted public attention by his perilous journey from Morocco to Tripoli by Tafilet, Tuat and Ghadames, performed his great journey to Bornou, and successfully crossed the African Continent from Tripoli on the Mediterranean to Lagos at the bottom of the Gulf of Guinea. This memorable expedition, one of the most daring and most profitable of this century, was followed by that of Dr. Nachtigal, who, in 1870, carried to the Sultan of Bornou presents from the King of Prussia in recognition of the services rendered by that sovereign to Barth, to Vogel, and to Rohlfs. During the following years, Nachtigal continued his explorations in the different states bordering on Lake Chad, and, thanks to him, the geography of these countries has made sensible progress. He was also the first European who, by the route from Murzook to Kuka, penetrated, in spite of the greatest dangers, into the country of the Tibboo Reskadé and visited Tibesti. He arrived in Egypt at the close of 1874, after having crossed the Wadai (that inhospitable land where Vogel and Beurmann had perished),

Darfur, and Kordofan, and thus connected his discoveries with those of the explorers of the Valley of the Nile. This expedition, extending over five years, is one of the most remarkable that has been performed in our times. It has placed Dr. Nachtigal in the first rank of African travellers, and opened up new prospects to such of them as shall hereafter take the Egyptian possessions for their basis of operations.

Egypt, since the reign of Mahomet Ali, has taken an exceptional position amongst the African states. When we look at the incurable decrepitude under which the Turkish Empire in Europe is sinking, she seems to be destined to inherit a very essential portion of the succession. The sword of General Bonaparte seems to have been the magic wand which has aroused from its tomb of thirty centuries the genius of Ancient Egypt. Thanks to the initiative of a series of princes who have been able, in more ways than one, to disentangle themselves from the narrow circle of Mohammedanism; thanks to the assistance of a host of men of administrative skill collected from every European nation, the Valley of the Nile has assumed quite a modern aspect. A regular service of steam-boats has been organised on the river up to the first cataract at Syene, and boats provided with every European comfort, every year convey thousands of tourists up to this point. Locomotives whistle at the foot of the Pyramids, and soon they will penetrate even into the desert, thanks to the contrivance of Fowler, the engineer, who has undertaken to construct a railway from the second cataract in Nubia as far as Khartoom, across the steppe of Bejuda, over an extent of nearly 200 leagues. At present Egypt possesses 1068 miles of railway line. At the north-east extremity of the country, the importance of the Isthmus of Suez is increasing year by year, and recent transactions have brought afresh into notice its high importance in view of the political changes of which the East may soon become the arena.

This revival of Egypt, with the territorial ambitions which it could not fail to excite, has come powerfully to the aid of the advancement of African geography. The government of the Khedive, especially, has lent a generous and unfailing support to those daring missionaries of science, who took his states as the point of departure of their explorations. The scantly hospitable reception recently given to the Italian expedition of the Marquis Antinori is an event as rare as it is regretable.

The determination of the basin of the Nile, and especially the search for its sources, have for a long time been and continue still to be the predominant aim of all enterprises. These have taken two directions, corresponding to the two branches of the Nile, which unite their waters at Khartoom, a city of 40,000 souls, the commercial metropolis of Eastern Soudan and the point of connection between Egypt and Central Africa. The eastern branch is called the Blue Nile (Bahr-el-Asrah), the west is called the White Nile (Bahr-el-Abiad).

At the close of last century the English traveller, Bruce, determined the sources of the Blue Nile. The system of its waters and the configuration of the Abyssinian plateau have been ascertained since in the most complete manner by two Frenchmen, Lefebvre, whose journey was made in 1839–43, and Lejean, who travelled through Abyssinia in 1862-64. The English expedition has made every one acquainted with this sort of African Switzerland, where the Christianity and the observances of the middle ages have been maintained down to our own times.

The Western system of the Nile is by far the more important of the two. The exploration of it began in the course of this century with the Swiss traveller, Burckhardt, who, in 1812–14, at the expense of the London African Society, traversed Nubia, and died at the time when he was about to enter the Libyan Desert with the view of reaching Fezzan. His immediate successor was a Frenchman, François Cailliaud, who penetrated into Upper Nubia as far as the tenth degree of latitude. This journey, which was made in 1819–22, gave a strong impulse to the study of Egyptian archæology. In 1819–41 Mahomet Ali sent two great expeditions to the Upper Nile. The first reached the sixth degree of latitude, and the second went as far as Gondokoro. About the same time the Austrian traveller, Russegger, visited the countries of Dar Nubar and of Takale, south of Kordofan, and enriched geographical science with some notable discoveries. (1837.)

At this period religious enthusiasm took its place by the side of scientific zeal. Catholic Missions were founded at Khartoom (1848), at Gondokoro (1851), and at St. Croix (1855), the object being to diffuse Christianity among the negro tribes and to put a check to the traffic in slaves. This attempt was not successful. The hostility of the slave dealers, famine, and, above all, fever, decimated the missionaries to so cruel an extent, that, in spite of their heroic devotedness, they finally abandoned an undertaking which, for science, at any rate, had not been unfruitful.

Protestant missions had scarcely better success in this region, but at another point they gave rise to an extraordinary impulse. In 1848 and 1849 the German missionaries Rebmann and Krapf discovered to the north of Zanzibar and nearly under the line two lofty mountains covered with perpetual snow, which they believed to be Ptolemy's Mountains of the Moon and the probable site of the sources of the Nile. This discovery at once stimulated the zeal of explorers in an exceptional manner. It afforded a glimpse of the possibility of penetrating southward to the Valley of the Nile, and of arriving by this new route at the solution of the problem.

Two officers of the Indian army, Captains Burton and Speke, received from the Geographical Society of London the charge of attempting this great enterprize. In 1857 they started from Zanzibar, pushed straight into the interior, and on the 13th of February, 1858, reached the shore of Lake Tanganyika. It was a day of mark in the annals of African exploration. After crossing the lake in its breadth, the two travellers separated. Speke turned his steps alone northward, and reached in this direction the southern shore of a second vast reservoir named by the natives Ukerewe, but which Speke baptized with the name of the Queen of England (Victoria Nyanza). Convinced that he had now found the true source of the Nile, Speke soon set out again, accompanied by Captain Grant. In 1861 the expedition again found itself near the Victoria, skirting it to the westward, but without perceiving another great lake in the neighbourhood, and penetrated into the country of Uganda, whose king, Mtesa, received them with great cordiality. On the northern shore of the lake, Speke and Grant discovered the outlet which, from that moment, they signalised as the head stream of the Nile. Although they were unable to follow its downward course continuously, the statements of the two English travellers have received a striking verification from subsequent expeditions, especially those of Colonel Long (1874), and of Stanley (1875). At Gondokoro, on their way back, Speke and Grant met Samuel Baker, who, with his heroic wife, had just undertaken the same exploration in a contrary direction. The meeting of the two expeditions was like a prophecy that the solution of the great problem was at hand.

In pursuing his course southwards, Baker again struck the Nile at the Falls of Karuma, a point from which his predecessors had diverged from the river, and he found that the river discharged itself into a second vast basin, the Mwutan, to which he gave the name of Albert Nyanza. This was in March, 1864. Although Baker saw only a small part of the shore of this lake, and had not found the outlet, the main system of the Nile was, from that time, almost settled.

These great discoveries, while they stimulated the ardour of scientific men and travellers, at the same time gave birth to vast political plans. The concentration of all the territories composing the immense basin of the Nile under the sceptre of the Viceroy of Egypt, was a notion conceived at Cairo, the execution of which rapidly passed into the domain of facts. In 1870, Samuel Baker started at the head of a small *corps d'armée* with the double mission of extending the authority of the Khedive as far as the lakes and of putting down the slave trade. This expedition, which lasted till 1873, and cost the Egyptian treasury the enormous sum of twenty-six millions of francs, only partly effected its object. In 1874, Colonel Gordon was charged to take it up on another footing. This campaign, which is not yet entirely completed, has already produced notable results. The dominion of the viceroy has acquired a solid basis in these countries, and at the same time the attempt to carry a steamer by the Nile as far as the Mwutan has been crowned with success. One member of the expedition, an engineer named Gessi, has just entered the lake by its northern outlet and made the circuit of the lake. The course of the White Nile is thus determined in a definite manner. Another traveller, renowned for his daring as much as for the success of his enterprises, the American, Stanley, has completed at another point this collection of discoveries. He carried a boat from the east coast up to Lake Victoria, and thus succeeded in making the circumnavigation of this grand reservoir, which receives ten rivers, and measures more than 960 miles in circuit. After a prolonged residence with the King of Uganda, he is now prosecuting his explorations towards the west.

In this direction, in fact, there lies another vast field for investigation. What is wanted is to trace westwards the line of hills which form the boundary of the basin of the White Nile, and to ascertain the system of its numerous affluents. Besides, in this direction, a meeting might be effected with travellers who had been engaged in the exploration of the central part of the Soudan, and thus observations made by those who had started from opposite points would be connected. Here, one after the other, we fall in with the Italians

Miani and Marquis Antinori, who, in 1860, travelled along the shores of the Bahr-el-Gazal and the Djur; the Frenchmen, Lejean and Pency, who visited the same regions in 1861; the English Consul Petherick, who, in his repeated excursions between 1848–1863, penetrated southward as far as the country of the Niam-Niam, where the Italian, Piaggia, took up his abode for a whole year (1864). Two Germans, Th. von Heuglin, and the botanist Steudner, which latter died in the course of the expedition, pushed their explorations beyond the Bahr-el-Gazal and the Djur as far as into the Dar Fertit. All these expeditions led to the remarkable journey of Dr. Schweinfurth, who, starting from Khartoom, in 1869, reached 3° 35' of north latitude across the country of the Niam-Niam and the Monbuttu. He described this previously unknown people, reached the ridge of the mountains (not very high, by the way) which separates the basin of the Nile from that of the Chad, and discovered on its western side the still mysterious river which he calls the Uelle. When he reached this point, although the courage of the daring traveller did not fail him, the exhaustion of his resources compelled him to return. With 40,000 francs more at his disposal, he believes that he would have been able to lead his men into the heart of the Soudan, where he would, perhaps, have met with Dr. Nachtigal. A worthy rival of these two men, the Austrian, Marno, who in 1872 had reached the south of Abyssinia as far as the country of the Galla, has made a reconnaissance to the left of the White Nile in the direction of the countries which Schweinfurth has reached by another road (1875). Here a field of research presents itself which is as extensive as it is new; the very centre of equatorial Africa now challenges the courage and the curiosity of explorers.

This vast unknown region of the central plateau, whose northern boundary the expeditions into the Soudan and the Valley of the Nile now make to range between two and ten degrees of north latitude, has not been free from a considerable number of attempts on its other frontiers. The Portuguese expeditions to these parts, some time ago now, have been of greater importance than is generally supposed. The great states of the Casembe and of the Muata Yamvo, which are only now beginning to emerge from obscurity, were travelled over during the first half of this century by a whole series of Portuguese explorers, who, starting from the west coast, reached the eastern limit of the plateau. These were Lacerda, who died on the field of his researches (1798); the Pombeiros (1808–10); Monteiro (1831) and Graça (1843–46). Ladislas Magyar, whose union with a native princess of Bihé places him in a peculiar position amongst his rivals, also visited these countries in 1850.

On the west coast, the English Captain, Tuckey, ascended the Congo in 1816, but without succeeding in passing the cataracts, and died under the pernicious influences of the climate. Du Chaillu, in 1856 and 1864, explored successively the mouths of the Gaboon and Ogowé, and penetrated, south of the latter river, 222 miles into the interior of the continent. After him the English missionary, Walker, and the French travellers, Marche and the Marquis de Compiègne, followed up the exploration of the Ogowé. These last made their way, in 1874, to beyond the Falls of Boué, the farthest point hitherto reached by Europeans.

At the bottom of the Bay of Biafra, Burton, in 1860, made the ascent of the gigantic Cameroon's Peak; while, on the opposite side of the African Continent, not far from the East Coast, Baron von der Decken, about the same period, ascended the still higher summit of Kilimanjaro, and died, in 1865, in attempting to ascend the River Juba.

Other interesting expeditions have made Southern Africa their starting points. The German zoologist, Fritsch, passed three years (1864–66) in the Orange Republic and among the Bechuanas, and collected in his journeys the materials of his learned work on the races of South Africa. In 1869 Ed. Mohr undertook his journey to the great cataract of the Zambesi. C. Mauch at the same time travelled over the Transvaal and the kingdom of Mosilikatse; he discovered the auriferous deposits of Tati, made his way, in 1872, throughout the whole of the south-east region, and discovered, in the twentieth degree of latitude, the remarkable ruins of Zimbabé. But one pre-eminently illustrious name stands high above those of all the travellers, who, in this part of the world, were his rivals or successors. David Livingstone occupies a place by himself in the history of African discovery. During more than thirty years, this admirable man fulfilled, with untiring zeal and superhuman energy, the double apostolate of the Gospel and of science. He singly traversed from south to north, and from west to east, one half of the African Continent, which had, in a manner, become to him a second country.

The travels of Livingstone began in 1840, in the English mission of Kuruman, among the Bechuanas. In 1845 they led him to the shores of Lake Ngami, the first of the great inland lakes discovered in Africa. His explorations extended, at that time, over the territories north of the Cape in which the Transvaal Republic has since been founded. Between 1853 and 1856, he accomplished the first of his great expeditions. He advanced northward towards the upper course of the Zambesi, and discovered its magnificent falls, even more imposing than those of the Niagara, visited the region of the sources of that river, and thence pushed westwards as far as Loanda, on the Atlantic coast. From this point he retraced his steps, and crossed

Africa throughout its breadth, coming out at Quilimane, on the Indian Ocean. Between 1858 and 1861, he accomplished a series of journeys which enabled him to determine the basin of the Zambesi, whose lower course he explored; he then ascended, across a succession of cataracts, its affluent, the Shiré, and discovered that this river was but the channel of discharge of an immense reservoir, the Lake Nyassa.

After a short interruption, during which he revisited England, Livingstone undertook, in 1866, his third and last expedition. Starting from the mouth of the Rovuma, he passed the end of the Nyassa, leaving it to the south, and penetrated the unknown country extending to the west of that basin. There he fell in with a new series of great lakes, the Bangweolo, the Moero, the Kamolondo, united by a mighty watercourse, the Lualaba or Luapula, which Livingstone, by mistake, took for the upper source of the Nile, but which later discoveries have connected with the systems of the Congo. In 1869, he reached Lake Tanganyika, which he partly traversed, and then turned westward and reached Nyangwe, the northern limit of his explorations.

He returned exhausted and ill to Ujiji, where, in the autumn of 1871, he met Stanley, who had been sent out to seek him; for, several times during the previous five years, the report of his death had been circulated in Europe. While Stanley returned to the coast, Livingstone, recomforted and reprovided with fresh means, skirted the east bank of the Tanganyika, and again plunged into the interior; he completed his investigations at different points, but before long, the fever contracted in the marshes under torrents of rain again laid hold of him, never to quit him more. At the beginning of 1873, he made the tour of Lake Bangweolo, and reached its southern shore. There he expired on the night of the 1st of May, under a shed improvised by his followers: in the morning he was found kneeling at the foot of his bed. History contains few pages more touching, or of a more sublime character, than the simple narrative of this silent and solitary death of a great man, the martyr to a great cause.

In this same year in which Livingstone died two expeditions started from England to seek traces of him.

One under the command of **Lieutenant Grandy, R.N.**, took the coast of Congo as its base of operations, but did not succeed. The second, also placed under the direction of a naval officer, Lieutenant Cameron, then twenty-eight years of age, produced results of extreme importance. Guided by the counsels of a man of high stamp, Sir Bartle Frere, Cameron started from Zanzibar at the close of 1873. At Kaseh, halfway to Tanganyika, he met the escort of Livingstone's attendants bringing back the remains of their master. After taking every step for insuring the transport of these precious remains, and the preservation of the papers of the illustrious traveller, Cameron resolutely went on his way. On the 2nd of February he reached Tanganyika, which he examined throughout its extent, and of which he made an exact map. In the course of his operations, he discovered the outlet of the lake, the Lukuga, which flows west and joins the Lualaba. This discovery decided Cameron on descending this river, and thus continuing the work of Livingstone. He reached Nyangwe, but there the hostility of a native chief compelled him to direct his steps south-west. In this direction he crossed the populous states of the Balunda, determined the system of affluents on the left shore of the Congo, and came out on the Atlantic in November, 1875, in the neighbourhood of Benguela. This memorable expedition, which has enriched science with eighty-five astronomical determinations of position, and 3,718 observations of altitude, was worthy of Livingstone, whose conception had led to the undertaking. Its success has been received throughout Europe with a well deserved feeling of admiration.

While we write these lines, new efforts are being set in motion. Germany is organising, under the probable direction of Ed. Mohr, a campaign of exploration which will take up, on the coast of Loango, the work commenced in 1873 by Dr. Güssfeldt, with the assistance of Major Homeyer, Dr. Lenz, Lieutenant Lux and other scientific men. France has expeditions in course of execution on the Ogowé: Italy has sent, under the command of Marquis Antinori, an expedition, the success of which is now very doubtful, but which proposed to go from Zeila, on the Gulf of Aden, to Lake Victoria, across the Galla Country.

England, absorbed at the present moment in its enterprise to the North Pole,* will not be long in bringing back its attention to Africa. Grave interests invite her thoughts in this direction.

The essential results of the principal journeys which have just been mentioned are brought together synoptically in the interesting map of Africa, published by the learned German geographer, H. Kiepert, in 1874, in vol. viii. of the *Zeitschrift* of the Geographical Society of Berlin. The tints employed show at the same time the part which appertains to the different nationalities of Europe in this great work of exploration, which has unhappily counted so many martyrs. But if the sacrifices have been cruel, at least they have not been fruitless. An idea may be formed of the progress accomplished by comparing the map of Kiepert with the description of the African Continent given in 1822 by Carl Ritter in his 'Géographie comparée,' which, it is true, in spite of the gaps in it, remains a monument of genius and knowledge. It is verily a new world which

* The expedition to the Pole returned to England on the 27th of October, 1876.

is opened up to the activity of mankind. Doubtless many localities still continue to be blanks on our maps. There still remains about a quarter of Africa to examine and describe; but so great has been the impulse communicated to research, that we may venture to hope that this century will not close without seeing the completion of this vast undertaking, especially if it should prove possible to place the enterprises of travellers on a footing which is at the same time broader and safer.

CHAPTER II.

A GLANCE AT THE PHYSICAL GEOGRAPHY OF AFRICA —ITS OROGRAPHICAL AND HYDROGRAPHICAL SYSTEMS —ITS CLIMATE AND PRODUCTS.

IN its general outline, Africa presents the form of a vast triangle, especially if we include the peninsula of Arabia, which is a natural dependency of it. Since the Isthmus of Suez has given place to a canal of seventy-six miles in length, it has become an entirely separated island. Its greatest vertical length, from Cape Blanco to Cape Agulhas, is 4809 miles; its greatest breadth, from Cape Verde to Cape Guardafui, 4674 miles; its total superficial measurement is nearly 18,000,000 of square miles. A simple glance at the map of this continent immediately shows one of the most prominent characteristics of its conformation. The contour of the African coast follows straight lines. It has no deep indentations, except the Syrtes on the north, and the Gulf of Guinea on the west, and these gulfs themselves have no spacious healthy bays. The seaboard of Africa is in proportion three times less extensive than that of Europe. If we add to this characteristic the elevation of the ground in the immediate neighbourhood of the coast, and nearly always parallel to it, it is easy to recognise the causes of the long isolation of Africa. Draw along the eastern shore of South America a chain of mountains parallel to the Andes, and the physical conditions of Africa are immediately reproduced: the low marshy coasts, at unequal distances, but always near the ocean; a vast central plateau traversed by numerous depressions, sometimes transverse, sometimes following the direction of the range; water-courses, sometimes insignificant like those of Algeria, Morocco, and the Cape, sometimes singularly imposing and extensive, but reaching the sea only by a succession of cataracts which present extreme difficulties to navigation. Such is, in brief, the picture of Africa, and these facts supply, in many respects, the explanation of its past history.

As regards the relief of its surface, the African Continent presents the most violent contrasts. In spite of the gaps which still exist in our knowledge of this branch of the subject, seven mountain systems are discernible, four of which are parallel, and three perpendicular to the equator.

On the north is the chain of the Atlas, stretching S.S.W. to N.N.E., from Agadir on the Atlantic to Tunis, where it descends perpendicularly to the Mediterranean. It reaches its greatest height in Morocco, at Miltsin, viz. 11,400 feet, and in the south of Algeria it again rises to 7493 feet.

Behind the Atlas range and the plateaux of Hamadan and Barka, which continue it eastwards, stretches from the Atlantic to the Nile, over an average breadth of 720 miles, the immense desert of the Sahara, the second rampart which has so long fenced off the interior of Africa against the investigations of science. Now that a number of travellers, at the head of whom we must quote Barth, Rohlfs, Duveyrier, and Nachtigal, have penetrated it in different directions, the Sahara is seen under a new aspect. It is no longer the uniform and deep depression, the moving and sterile bed of a dried-up sea which we always imagined it; it is a vast plain, with its valleys and mountains, containing tribes, not nomadic only, but stationary also, and covered with vegetation wherever the action of rain can make itself felt. The character of the sandy, arid desert prevails in the west; that of the occasionally verdant and occasionally rocky steppe, towards the east. The Sahara presents some deep depressions; such as that of El Juf, in the south of Morocco, where not long ago it was contemplated to admit the Atlantic by a canal; that of Wad Righ, in the south of Algeria, descends sensibly like that of Libya, below the level of the Mediterranean: the latter falls as low as 340 feet. Everywhere else the country rather presents the form of plateaux intersected by valleys; that of Fezzan reaches 1476 feet. Some of these isolated plateaux become, as they rise, picturesque oases: such are the mountainous groups of Asgar (4265 feet); of Air (4757 feet); of Anahef (5249 feet). The islet of Tibesti, visited by Dr. Nachtigal for the first time in 1870, and which is perhaps the most inhospitable spot in the Sahara, forms its culminating point. It is as much as 8530 feet high.

At the opposite extremity of Africa stands the enormous Cape range of mountains, which sinks by a succession of three terraces towards the southern point of the continent. The seaboard, the plain of the Karroos (3280 feet), and the lofty Orange plateau, which developes itself into the Roggeveld, the Nieuweveld and the Schneeberg (5249 feet) form the layers. This system is continued in Caffraria and Natal, where it abuts on the Drakenberg. Imposing peaks prevail in it; the Compas (8800 feet), on the Cape side, the Cathkin (10,032 feet), in the colony of Natal: everywhere the slopes are abrupt, and admit access to the interior only by narrow passes.

With this system correspond, but at much lower elevations, the heights which separate the basins of the Orange River and the Limpopo from that of the Zambesi. Their principal features are the arid and desert plateau of Kalahari, with its two counter-forts of Owahcrero (8530 feet) to the west, and the mountains of Matoppo (7217 feet) to the east. Between these two ranges is the hollow which forms the Lake Ngami. Beyond stretches a country of Alpine plateaux travelled over in every direction by Livingstone. The prevailing characteristic of this region, which is but of moderate and inconsiderable elevation, is its extreme wealth of water. The Zambesi and its numerous affluents spread around fertility and life. In the rainy season, the whole zone corresponding with the upper and middle course of the Zambesi is converted into a lake, and the inundation extends even beyond the watershed into the basin of the Congo. This circumstance it was that suggested to Cameron the idea that it would be possible to unite these two river-systems by a canal.

The basin of the Zambesi is inclosed on the north by the plateau of Lobisa, which is continued westwards by the Muxinga chain. The plateau, more than 6560 feet high, sinking suddenly to the east, forms, at an altitude of 1522 feet, the vast hollow of Lake Nyassa. Westward the slope descends gently by a series of terraces. Its culminating point in that direction is in the Mountains of Mossamba in the province of Benguela. This elevation constitutes, in a range of about 1500 miles, the line of separation between the waters which fall into the Atlantic on the one side, and into the Indian Ocean on the other. The abundance of river heads, the majority of which become large rivers, is in this part extraordinary. Livingstone counted thirty-two over a distance of sixty-six miles. Travellers have compared the numberless meshes of this hydrographical net-work to the radiations traced on our windows by the frost on winter nights.

Between this mountain-system on the south, and the plateaux of the Sahara on the north, lies Central Africa, which has now become the leading object of scientific exploration. It is an elevated mass of an extent unrivalled on the globe, and presenting the general aspect of a trapezium; the inclination of the land is from east to west. It is either bordered or traversed by lofty plateaux, from which spring up isolated mountains, reckoned amongst the highest on earth, from whose sides descend the most majestic rivers, while in the intervals between them lie spread out the most gigantic lakes in the world.

Three lines of heights intersect the central plateau

of Africa, from south to north. The first constitutes the eastern border. It begins near the seventh degree of south latitude, runs parallel to the coast, and expands itself into the enormous Abyssinian range, from which the Arabian chain detaches itself towards the north. This imposing rampart serves as the watershed to three seas; it reaches its culminating point nearly under the equator, in Kilimanjaro (20,065 feet), and Kenia (20,000 feet), the summits of which, covered with eternal snow, are not only the loftiest in Africa, but have no equal in Europe, and are rarely surpassed in Asia.* The average altitude of the chain is from 5900 to 6890 feet; towards the west it developes itself into a plateau, the two enormous depressions of which form, one northward at an elevation of 3766 feet, the immense lake, Victoria Nyanza, the original reservoir of the Nile, the other southward, at an elevation of 2710 feet, the not less considerable basin of the Tanganyika, which the recent discoveries of Cameron

---

* Mont Blanc the highest summit in Europe, is 15,780 feet high. The highest in the world is Mount Everest in the Himalayas, which is 29,000 feet high.

have connected with the river system of the Congo. Westward of this line, a second presents itself, with analogous average altitudes; it follows the west bank of the Tanganyika, passes between the two lakes, Victoria and Albert Nyanza, where its culminating point presents itself in Mfumbiro (10,825 feet). There it sinks eastwards, forming a succession of plateaux; westwards it joins on to the Blue Mountains of Baker, and thence passes to the Atlantic Ocean, separating the respective basins of Lake Chad, of the Nile, of the Ogowé, and of the Congo; raises, in Adamawa, the imposing peaks of Mindif (6561 feet) and of Atlantika (9840 feet), and terminates, at the bottom of the Bay of Biafra, in the colossal Peak of Cameroons (10,770 feet).

The third chain of mountains of Central Africa is that which forms the western border of the plateau. It extends, under the successive names of Sierra de Cristal, Sierra Cumplida, Sierra Fria, etc., across the provinces of Loango, Angola, and Benguela, where it joins on to the range of the Mossamba Mountains. Its distance from the coast varies from 132 to 198 miles; the altitude, which follows a decreasing scale in the direction of south to north, descends from 4493 to 656 feet. It is in clearing this rampart that the great rivers of West Africa form those cataracts which have hitherto prevented travellers from penetrating by these ways into the heart of the country. The line of heights which separates the coast of Guinea from the Soudan, and known under the name of the Kong Mountains, if we take the Cameroons as the common point of junction, may be regarded as the western prolongation of this chain. In its northern course, this coast-line chain expands itself into the Senegambian range, the last counter-forts of which sink towards the Sahara and form the dividing line between the waters of the Niger, the Senegal, and the Gambia.

The orographical description of the African Continent directly furnishes the key to the distribution of its waters. The worse provided Northern Africa is, in this respect, the greater is the superabundance in Central Africa. The latter forms the base of nearly the whole fluvial system, covering a surface of about 3,600,000 square miles. It contains the sources of three enormous water-courses, the first of which is the unique tributary of the Mediterranean, and the two others, the principal affluents, one of the Atlantic, and the other of the Indian Ocean. These are the Nile, the Congo, and the Zambesi.

The Nile is the king of the rivers of the terrestrial globe. The distance in a straight line from its sources to its mouth, is 2340 miles, which supposes a real length, exceeding that of the Mississippi, Missouri, and Amazons. According to the calculations of Schweinfurth, its fluvial basin extends over a surface of 4,956,000 square miles; the basin of the Amazon measures no more than 4,200,000; that of the Mississippi scarcely exceeds 2,000,000 square miles. The source of this gigantic artery, Lake Ukereme or Victoria Nyanza, is itself an immense reservoir fed by numerous watercourses. The height of this reservoir is 3766 feet, and its surface measures 50,400 square miles, that is to say, an extent nearly triple that of Belgium. The Nile issues from the northern side of this basin, with a breadth of 393 feet, and descends by a series of falls into a second reservoir, the Mwutan or Albert Nyanza, but only traverses its northern part. The Mwutan, according to the most recent observations, is at an elevation of 2198 feet above the level of the sea; it measures 132 miles in length, and from twenty-one to fifty-four in breadth. At its exit from this second lake, the river, which is there 1443 feet broad, takes the name of the White Nile (Bahr-el-Abiad). It crosses an uneven country, and its bed is strewed with rocks, which, with the rapids, forbid all navigation. It receives a multitude of affluents, the principal of which are the Bahr-el-Gazal on the left, and the Sobat, which descends from the Abyssinian plateau, on the right. From Gondokoro, the Nile continues to be navigable: but here commences a marshy hollow, which, in the rainy season, converts this region into a vast lake covered with impenetrable reeds. The putrid miasmas which arise from these submerged and hot lands, have made numerous victims amongst travellers and missionaries.

Beyond the point of junction with the Bahr-el-Gazal, the Nile takes its northward direction, but not without describing many curves; it is dotted with islets and floating masses of vegetation as far as Khartoom, where it receives the eastern branch which, under the name of Blue Nile (Bahr-el-Asrak), brings it the rich tribute of the Abyssinian waters. Farther down it is joined by another considerable affluent, the Atbara or Takazze, also descending from the eastern plateau. It is the diluvian rains falling every year on these high grounds which constitutes the principal cause of the periodical rises of the Nile; the rich mud which fertilises the Egyptian Valley is a present from Abyssinia.

From Khartoom, the capital of the Egyptian Soudan, and the point of departure of the scientific expeditions which penetrate Africa from the north-east, the river flows northwards, describing vast curves across Nubia. The cataracts which occur again in this second half of its course as far as Assouan, only partially interfere with navigation. At Cairo the Nile splits and throws itself into the Mediterranean by several branches, the principal of which are those of Damietta and Rosetta.

For length of course and volume of water the Congo takes rank immediately after the Nile. Like it, it is a giant river at its mouth. It measures nearly six miles in breadth, and it is as much as 1312 feet deep. Such is the force of the current that, at a distance of sixty miles out at sea, its waters are not entirely blended with those of the ocean, and at fifteen miles from the coast the water is quite fresh. The enormous outflow of the Congo (167,000 cubic feet per second) supposes a hydrographical basin of extreme abundance. Until recent times, its lower course was only known as far as Yellali, but the explorations of Livingstone and Cameron have changed the aspect of things.

The first of these travellers discovered in the heart of Central Africa, and ascertained the sources of, the River Lualaba, which from many indications is regarded as the upper course of the Congo. This river, which under the name of Chambeze, descends from the western slope of the plateau of Lobisa, traverses a series of great lakes, the Bangweolo, the Moero, and the Kamolondo, in stages one above the other, and fed by numerous streams. The region surrounding them is one of excessive humidity, and has been compared to a sponge constantly charged with water. At every two or three miles Livingstone had to cross a river. At Nyangwe, the northernmost point reached by this traveller, and beyond which Cameron was not able to penetrate, the Lualaba, after a course of more than 180 miles, presents a breadth of from 5250 to 5905 feet, and a depth of from nine to thirteen feet. The number of its affluents is considerable; the most important of all perhaps is the Lukuga, recently discovered by Cameron. This river pours into the Lualaba the waters of the vast reservoir of Tanganyika, the first of the great lakes encountered by Burton and Speke in their expedition of 1858. The Tanganyika, at an elevation of 2710 feet, measures 402 miles in length, and from twelve to sixty-six miles in breadth with 22,320 square miles of superficies. The Lukuga is its only outlet, and this fact would suffice to account for the enormous volume of water which the Congo discharges at its mouth. Supposing, however, that later researches confirm the identity of the Lualaba with the Congo—of which there can be little doubt—the middle course of the river would still remain to be determined. It is to this part of its basin that the two great affluents of Kassabi and Quango belong, the sources of which have been recently explored by Cameron.

The Zambesi, the entire examination of which remains one of Livingstone's great titles to glory, is the third of the colossal arteries which descend from Central Africa. The hydrographical network of which its upper course consists expands itself, between the Mossamba Mountains and the heights of Ovaherero, over a terrace superabundantly watered; the Liba which issues from Lake Dilolo (4265 feet in elevation), the Liambey, the name of which it for some time bears, and the Chobe are here the principal affluents. When it reaches the plateau of the Batokas, it falls in a mass from a height of 4757 feet, forming the celebrated fall called by the natives Mosiwatunja, which means "thundering smoke," but to which Livingstone gave the name of Victoria Falls. Downwards, from this point, the river is deeply embosomed in a narrow valley, overleaps the pass of Lupate, and receives the Shiré, which brings it across one of the roughest of roads, the tribute of the waters of Lake Nyassa, another large inland basin, lying 1522 feet above the level of the sea, and equal in extent to half of Tanganyika. Its length is, in fact, 210 miles, and its average breadth thirty miles, and its superficies 9000 square miles. On nearing the sea-coast, the Zambesi, after having formed numerous cataracts, suddenly widens its banks, and falls in manifold branches into the Indian Ocean between Quilimane and Luabo.

Besides these three water-courses of incomparable power, Africa presents a fourth, which is but little inferior to them; viz., the Niger. This river, the exploration of which was for a long time the passion of travellers, is far from being completely known even now. In its whole length, estimated at 2220 miles, it presents many analogies with the Nile, the physical conditions of which it reproduces in an inverse sense, on the opposite side of the African Continent. It rises in the same mountains whose opposite slope gives birth to the Senegal and Gambia, flows north-east as far as the edge of the Sahara near Timbuctoo, that great emporium of the Soudan so rarely visited even to this day; and from this point it describes a vast curve to the south-east across the rich and populous states of the Fellata. It is at their southern borders that the Niger receives its principal affluent, the

Chadda or Benué, an imposing river, of which the lower course only is known, and the further description of which remains, on account of the beauty of its banks, one of the most interesting problems of African geography. Beyond its confluence with the Benué, the Niger breaks up into a multitude of branches, and finishes its course in the Gulf of Guinea, forming a delta, sadly famous for its exceptional unhealthiness.

Between the basin of the Nile and that of the Niger, bordered on the north by the Sahara, and on the south by the central plateau of Africa, there is a vast depression, the bottom of which is occupied by Lake Chad. This large reservoir, of which Dr. Nachtigal has recently made the circuit, covers an approximate superficies of 6600 square miles, an extent which may be multiplied by five in the rainy season. On the south it receives a considerable affluent, the Sharé, which has not as yet been ascended to any great distance. Schweinfurth believes that he has discovered its upper course in the Welle, which descends from the western slope of the Blue

Mountains, and, not far from its sources, already has a breadth of 885 feet.

The limits of this work compel us here to close this summary picture of the water systems of Africa. In order to complete it, there would remain to be described the characteristics of the Senegal and Gambia, whose waters are gradually being opened to navigation under the auspices of France, which is in possession of the shores; the vast estuary of the Gaboon under the equator; the Ogowé which belongs to the system of Central Africa, and has only within the last few years come within the range of our positive knowledge; the Coanza and the Cunene, which debouch in the Portuguese possessions on the west coast, but are still almost entirely unknown; the Garib, or Orange, which, deeply embosomed in its bed, crosses, without fertilising, the northern plateau of the Cape; the Limpopo which, both on the west and on the north, forms the boundary of the Transvaal Republic; the Rufuma, the Lufiji, and the Juba, which water the east coast, but as yet are but little known to any distance from their mouths. The greater part of these arteries, moreover, present the characteristics common to all the great African rivers; viz., marshes or lakes in the region of the sources: rapids and cataracts in their middle course, and submerged deltas at their lower course. Periodical risings also are by no means a phenomenon peculiar to the Nile; they occur nearly everywhere: those of the Zambesi, for example, reach fifty-nine feet in the centre of the continent.

The astronomical position of Africa, combined with the system of its mountains and its waters, explains its climate. It is comparatively the hottest continent of the globe, four-fifths of its surface being under the torrid zone. Its great extension to the north of the equator, and the extent and slightness of elevation of the Sahara re-act on the temperature of a great part of Africa. The north coast has an average temperature of 12° Réaumur; to the south this figure rises to 16°. In the equatorial zone, the climate varies sensibly, in consequence of the height of the terraces and plateaux; the heat is not really excessive, except on the low and humid coasts in

Nubia and the Sahara, where the thermometer is often above 40° Réaumur. At the same time the difference between the temperature of the day and that of the night is considerable; under the influence of radiation it reaches sometimes 36°. This circumstance explains how even in these regions frost and snow are not altogether unknown. The thermal equator, which represents the maximum of the mean temperatures of the year (22° Réaumur), cuts Africa at the 6th degree of north latitude on the west coast, rises to the 15th degree in the interior, and touches the western coast under the 10th degree of north latitude. Most of the countries which it crosses are, nevertheless, on account of their elevation, habitable by Europeans; this is notably the case in most of the regions of the Soudan. The central plateau is not formidable, except in its marshy hollows, and the Cape, Caffraria and the Republics of the Boors enjoy everywhere a temperate and healthy climate.

With respect to the distribution of rain, Africa is divided into seven zones. In Algeria, Morocco, and Tripoli, it rains in winter, spring, and autumn, but never in summer. These same conditions are reproduced south of the 26th degree of south latitude: i.e., in Cape Colony, the Orange Republic, Caffraria, and Natal. The Sahara, Egypt, and Nubia know nothing of rain, except as a rare phenomenon. In Senegambia, the Soudan, and Guinea, on the north; in the country of the Hottentots, in the Transvaal, and the coast of Sofalá on the south, it only rains in summer. The region extending 4° on each side of the equator is visited by rains every month of the year, with the ordinary accompaniment of violent storms. Finally, in the zone comprised between the 4th and 16th degrees of south latitude (Angola, Benguela, the upper basins of the Congo and Zambesi, and Mozambique) it rains in summer and winter. In the countries where the rains are periodical, the revolution effected is startling: vast dried up and burnt tracts become covered, as by enchantment, with a luxurious vegetation.

The flora and fauna of Africa are of extreme richness and variety. The narratives of travellers abound with animated pictures of the splendours of the vegetation. The impenetrable virgin forests, the picturesque palm groves, the immense baobab, whose circumference reaches 160 feet, and whose age is counted by centuries, form the well-known elements of their descriptions. Africa, moreover, lends herself to all the growths of hot and temperate countries; she produces all the cereals of Europe, as well as dourah (Indian millet); common millet and rice; spices; oils and resins; coffee, sugar-cane, cotton; plants for dyeing (madder, indigo, orchil); and for medicine (aloes, senna, colombo, &c.): woods for building and for cabinet work (santal, ebony, pallissander or rosewood); a great variety of fruits (pineapples, figs, dates, oranges); and, lastly, the vine, which in several countries gives wonderful yields, while there is almost an unlimited field for its extension.

The African fauna is not less richly provided. In domestic species, it reproduces, especially in north and south Africa, all the European animals, as well as the camel, which is peculiar to the deserts and steppes of the north. Wild species abound. All the great races are there represented. The lion is met from Algeria to the Cape; the elephant, the rhinoceros, the hippopotamus, the buffalo, the antelope, and the gazelle are there in countless numbers. The ostrich runs over all the plains, and the crocodile is found in all the waters of tropical Africa. Serpents swarm; apes, among which the chimpanzee and the formidable gorilla of the western coast deserve special mention, are in legions. Insects, locusts, ants, termites; and, in the south, the tsetse fly are among the scourges of Africa, from their numbers, the ravages they make, and the tortures they inflict.

In the way of mineral products, one can scarcely catch a glimpse as yet at the resources of the African soil: a certainty however has been arrived at as to the presence of the precious metals, especially gold, of iron in great quantity, of copper, lead, sulphur, coal, and precious stones, particularly diamonds and emeralds.

The physical conditions thus summarily indicated enable us to form at least a vague idea of the infinite variety of the African landscape as soon as we have crossed the border of the Sahara on the north and that of the Kalahari on the south. Here it is the interminable savannah, with its tall grasses intermixed with tree-clumps; elsewhere it is the virgin forest which displays the matchless splendour of its forms and its colours under slender colonnades surmounted by a triple arch of verdure. Farther on, it is the Alpine type of nature reappearing with its lakes and its cascades, its valleys dotted with picturesque villages, its mountains with abrupt flanks over-towering vast plateaux; everywhere springs, rivers, reservoirs uniting and interblending the superabundant mass of their waters. Schweinfurth describes with admiration the country of Niam-Niam on the extreme limits of the Nile basin, and extols the richness of its appearance. Under the same latitude (10° north latitude), but in quite a different direction, Rohlfs calls the plateau of the Bautschi a real paradise; Stanley never tires of admiring the beauty of the countries lying behind Zanzibar. Linant de Bellefonds compares Uganda, with its splendid plantations of bananas, to the fairest countries of Italy. The magnificence of the basin of the Lualaba inspires Livingstone with enthusiasm, even when already a dying man. Lastly, Cameron describes the interior of Central Africa as a country almost always marvellous, healthy, and of incredible richness.

These smiling pictures have, it is true, dark shadows. The narratives of travellers testify at every page to the sufferings which have to be endured, and the dangers which have to be defied, in order to reach these distant lands and wrest from them their secrets. How many of them have paid with their lives for the distinguished discoveries which have immortalised them! Whatever contrivance may be conceived for rendering their task more easy, it would be rash to hope that the four millions of square miles which remain to be discovered in Central Africa, will be won to our knowledge without new and cruel sacrifices. But, on the other hand, it is also certain that Africa does not present to Europeans any obstacles more formidable than those which have had to be overcome in the two Americas, in India, and Java, or even in Australia. When this conviction shall have become general, a few well directed efforts will suffice to remove the last impediments to our enlightenment.

CHAPTER III.

ETHNOGRAPHY OF AFRICA—MORAL AND SOCIAL CONDITION OF THE NEGROES.

THE physical conformation of the African Continent has exercised a preponderating influence on the history and civilisation of the races that inhabit it. The idea which Carl Ritter made the basis of his celebrated 'Géographie comparée,' seems to have been suggested by the study of Africa, in which it found its first and most fruitful application. The regular and straight line of the coasts, the falls and rapids so frequent in its rivers, had the effect of concentrating on the sea-coast the activity of the native populations. These have all confined themselves to the first elements of the art of navigation. The ocean has never attracted them far from their shores, which have always been to them the extremity of the world. The Ancient

Egyptians themselves form no exception to this rule; they have never been a sea-going people.

To this cause of isolation has to be added the immense barrier of the Sahara, extending from the Valley of the Nile to the shores of the Atlantic, and whose arid solitudes, before the acclimatisation of the camel in Africa by the Ptolemies, no human being had ever dreamed of crossing. From these two facts it has resulted that, during the whole range of antiquity, the influence of civilising nations has been confined to the northern zone of Africa, and has not passed beyond the chain of the Atlas or the Valley of the Nile. These regions alone have been found to be in regular intercourse with Europe and Asia. In them has flourished the civilisation of Egypt, of Cyrenaica, of Carthage, and of the Roman provinces; and from them some few elements of refinement have penetrated among the races of the interior. Thus the art of casting iron, which has remained unknown to the aborigines of America, has little by little spread as far as the southern extremity of the continent, and has become a common inheritance.

These observations explain an interesting phenomenon which has been confirmed by all travellers: viz., that in regard to intellectual and social development, the African races follow on a decreasing scale in the direction from north to south and from east to west. The negroes of the west coast are the most backward amongst their congeners; the Bechuanas, in the immediate neighbourhood of the Cape, occupy, so to speak, the lowest scale in the hierarchy of races. There exist, very many indications of an ebbing of the races in these same directions. The more energetic and industrious tribes of the Soudan, of the Upper Nile, and of the Caffres, are constantly driving before them, towards the shores of the Atlantic, as well as towards the lofty and sterile plateaux extending northward of the Cape, the tribes which are inferior to themselves. Were it not for the comparatively limited density of the African population, and, above all, for the enormous losses inflicted by the slave trade, this movement would doubtless have produced more momentous disturbances.

With respect to ethnography, the inhabitants of

Africa range themselves in zones with an almost mathematical regularity. The whole of the north, down to the southern border of the Sahara, belongs to the Caucasian race. From the desert to the extremity of the tropical zone extends the country of the negro. Beyond that, hemmed in more and more by the European establishments of the Cape and of the Boors, the exhausted race of the Hottentots and the Bechuanas still holds on.

This last group is only of secondary importance. The tribes of which it is composed seem doomed to an early extinction. They lead a wandering life, the Bechuanas as hunters, the Hottentots as shepherds. Nevertheless, wretched as is their physical and social condition, and deep as is the degeneration of species that is evident amongst them, these races, in some respects, cannot fail to excite a very keen interest. Modern travellers have been struck, for example, with the beauty and remarkable amount of development of the idiom of the Hottentots, which exhibits astonishing analogies with the language of the Ancient Egyptians. It would doubtless be rash to found inferences on such a fact, but if we bring into connection with it the recent discovery due to C. Mauch, of the imposing ruins of Zimbabe, north-east of the country now inhabited by the Hottentots, we gain a perception of what an amount of perspectives, as yet unforeseen by science, may still be opened up by the study of Africa. But we must close this parenthesis in order to return to the two dominant groups of African races, each of which comprises several great subdivisions.

The Caucasians of Africa divide themselves into two main branches: those which speak the Hamitic language and those that speak the Semitic language. To the former category belong the Ancient Egyptians, whose race survives only in the insignificant residue of the Copts. The Libyans, who now bear the name of Berbers, are, on the other hand, in full existence, thanks to the Desert, which is their true domain. The Numidians, the Getulians, and the Moors, were the ancestors of that great family which now exists in Morocco (the Masig), in Algeria (the Kabyles and the Mosabites), in Tunis and the Oases, especially in the Western Sahara, where the Tuaregs are their most characteristic representatives. Groups of Berbers are found in Nubia, on the middle of the Nile, and the shores of the Red Sea; the Gallas, who inhabit the plains to the south of Abyssinia, perhaps even the Somauli, who occupy the extreme promontory of East Africa, are also branches of the same stock.

The Berbers generally have a clear complexion, with noble and stongly-marked features. They have preserved many of the elements of the physiognomy, manners, and culture of the Ancient Egyptians. The Tuaregs on the west, and the Gallas on the east, are the purest representatives of the Egyptian type. They are wandering tribes, warlike, and of an energetic and hardy character; they are by turn the protectors or the worst enemies of the caravans which convey the products of Central Africa across the desert. The Berber tribes have rarely founded states; their political development has been limited to the tribe.

The Caucasians of Semitic race are represented in Africa by three groups: the *Arabs*, who poured themselves like a torrent over Africa, driving northwards the Berbers of all the countries on the seaboard of the

Mediterranean and Atlantic, founding on the eastern coast the Sultanate of Zanzibar, imposing their language and propagating their religion throughout about half of the African Continent; the *Jews*, who have established little communities at different points of the northern zone, but have nowhere gained for themselves independence; and the *Abyssinians*, who, in spite of many vicissitudes, uphold on the lofty plateaux of their country a nationality which has often been threatened, and an appearance, scarcely recognisable, of Christianity.

In modern times, but especially in the nineteenth century, the Caucasian race on the soil of Africa has received accessions from a new source. European nations have begun to extend their possessions and their influence there, both on the continent and in the islands. The French in Algeria and Senegambia; the English on the coast of Guinea, at the Cape and at Natal; the Dutch in the two Southern Republics; the Portuguese in the Cape Verde Islands and the provinces of Angola, Benguela and Mozambique; the Spaniards, in the Canary Islands and Fernando Po, have founded

F

colonies, and commercial establishments, which, as centres of civilisation, cannot fail to extend their influence towards the interior of the continent. The hitherto surprisingly limited number, however, of colonists, and the obstacles to the extension of their intercourse with the natives, presented by the deserts and mountains at most of the points where they have established themselves, have been the causes why their presence has not produced all the results which might have been hoped for. If modern Egypt continues to develope itself in the path of progress introduced by its latest sovereigns, it may contribute in the most effectual manner to the work undertaken by the nations of Europe.

Behind the Desert of Sahara, from the Atlantic to the Upper Nile, stretches southwards the vast empire of the negroes. The line of transition is not so strongly defined as is commonly believed. Thus, the origin of the tribe of the Tibboo, or Teda, is a contested point, so uncertain do their physical characteristics appear. The same difficulties are met with in classifying the Fulbe, or Fellatas, which caused the learned

Münzinger to say that, "After attentive observation, the conscientious traveller is unable to distinguish where the negro type really commences, and gives up the belief in the absolute separation of the races."

Contemporary science has confirmed this assertion. A veritable revolution has been effected in the notions which for too long a time prevailed with respect to the populations of Central Africa. Till only quite recently, when negroes were spoken of, how many people looked upon them as quite inferior beings, leading a purely animal existence, strangers to every kind of cultivation, dwelling in the woods in separate groups, almost on a par with the monkeys, with which, indeed, sometimes people were not far from confounding them! Their physical type had become proverbial: an ovoid cranium, a low and retreating forehead, the jaws very prominent, the nose flat, the lips thick, the hair short and curly and resembling tufts of wool, a complexion black as ebony, the arms long, the feet flat, etc. Such were the characteristic marks of the race in general opinion, and even amongst authors.

Now it is of importance to show, that, according

to the concurrent testimony of all travellers, the combination of these traits is not to be found in any tribe, not even the lowest in the scale of the race. The typical negro, says Winwood Reade, is a rare exception. Among negroes, the complexion passes through the whole gamut of shades, from deep black and coppery red, to bright yellow, approaching nearly to white (the Fellata); the protrusion of the jaw and thickness of the lips disappear in a number of the tribes, and a good many of them have the nose straight and pointed; long, straight hair is not uncommon; and Schweinfurth has seen even blonde negroes. Travellers assert that they have frequently met with Greek profiles in Africa. Livingstone speaks highly of the plastic beauty of the Africans of Equatorial Africa. Speaking of one of their nations, he writes in his last journal: "They are a fine-looking race; I would back a company of Manyuema men to be far superior in shape of head, and generally in physical form too against the whole Anthropological Society. Many of the women are very light-coloured and very pretty."

This language is applied to a tribe living in the

heart of Africa, some degrees south of the equator, and is by no means an exception. We must therefore renounce old prejudices, and acknowledge that nature has not physically disgraced the negroes to the point of excluding them, in some sort, from the human family.

The negroes, whose total number is reckoned at one hundred and fifty millions of souls, form one single race, subdivided into two leading groups, which again break up into a multitude of inferior unities. These groups are:

Firstly: The negroes of the Soudan, which spread from Senegambia to the sources of the Nile, and descend southward as far as the fourth degree of north latitude.

Secondly: The Bantoo negroes, or Caffres, who occupy the whole of Central Africa, as far as the southern limits of the basin of the Zambesi, which they even overstep on the eastern side, where they advance towards the Cape.

The negroes of the Soudan present a great variety of types and of degrees of civilisation. The Fulbe, or

Fellatas, hold the first rank among them; their ethnographical derivation is uncertain; some even profess to discover in them a race distinct from that of the negroes. The Fellatas have a clear brown, sometimes olive complexion, aquiline nose, regular mouth, and hair generally long and silky: the physiognomy is noble, the build of the body vigorous, and, in all these respects, they are scarcely to be distinguished from the inhabitants of the southern countries of Europe. The moral character of these people answers to the idea suggested by their physical appearance. Courage, frankness, dignity of bearing, energy, and determination are their distinctive traits. Religious feeling is highly developed among the Fellatas: they are fanatical followers of Islamism, of which they are the indefatigable apostles among the Pagan tribes. They are fond of work, devoted to agriculture and the rearing of cattle, and successfully cultivate various branches of industry.

The number of the Fellatas is reckoned at from six to eight millions. Their principal establishment is in Senegambia, from the mouths of the Senegal to the lofty range from which flows the Niger. From this region they have spread, on one side, southwards, to the neighbourhood of the coast of Sierra Leone, and on the other, eastwards, into the basin of the Niger, where they have become the preponderant, if not exclusive, element. There they have founded the three considerable states of Massina, of which Timbuctoo (20,000 souls) is the principal city, Gando and Sokoto. Southeast, they extend as far as Adamawa, a province which no traveller has yet explored. Beyond the countries which they rule over, their influence makes itself felt in all the negro states of the basin of Lake Chad, and even in Darfur.

The Soudanian negroes, properly so called, of whom the Kanuri of Bornou are the typical representatives, differ sensibly from their neighbours in the west. They are tall and strong; the face is broad, the nose flat, the mouth large, and the physiognomy, in general, far from attractive. This physical conformation is not, however, uniform; the population of certain districts of Bornou even differ from it so widely, that the beauty of their women is renowned throughout the whole of North Africa. These negroes are gentle, indolent, and timid. The introduction of Islamism has divided them into two categories, the believers and the infidels.

Under the influence of this religious teaching, the social condition of the Mussulman Soudanians has undergone a transformation. They have founded a series of principalities more or less independent, reproducing in a tolerably faithful fashion the usual type of states ruled by the Koran. Four of these states surround Lake Chad: Bornou on the west, Kanem on the north, Wadai on the east, Bagirmi on the southeast. Two others, Darfur and Kordofan, lying at the eastern extremity of the Soudan, have just passed under the sovereignty of Egypt.

All these states are governed by absolute chiefs, who assume the title of Sultan; they possess a social hierarchy, strictly exclusive, small bodies of troops partially provided with fire-arms (the army of Bornou counts 30,000 men, the greater part cavalry), and chief towns, some of which, such as that of Bornou (Kuka), for example, contain not less than 60,000 souls. These capitals have regular streets and houses built either of wood or earth. Their handiwork, naturally primitive, has nevertheless, in some branches, not failed to produce notable results. The products of Europe reach as far as this by the Arab caravans from Morocco or Tripoli. With a wealth of soil that might be said to be inexhaustible, these countries unhappily, only give in return, ivory and ostrich feathers. Slavery, which is a universal institution there, paralyses the development of industry, by degrading labour; the traffic in men, which is the immediate consequence of slavery, has, in Africa, this natural result of rendering regular commerce impossible. The long sojourn which the latest German travellers, such as Barth, Rohlfs, and Nachtigal have made in the principalities of the Soudan, have initiated us into the minutest details of their organisation.

The Pagan negroes of this region have not reached the same point of cultivation as their Mussulman brethren; the Ashantees and Dahomians, however, hostile as they have shown themselves on various occasions to Europeans, have developed amongst themselves the rudiments of a civilisation. The state of Joruba, bordering on Dahomey to the west, contains towns, such as Ilori and Ibadan, the population of which amounts to between 70,000 and 100,000 souls. These large cities, which have regular streets, markets, and public squares, have extensive and active commercial connections.

The negroes of the Upper Nile, the Shilluks, the Dinkas, the Djurs, etc., are, in every respect, the least advanced among the Pagan negroes of the Soudan. The more deeply, however, we penetrate, on this side, into the heart of Africa, the more we shall find the social aspect of the populations exhibit a change. There, among others, we come upon tribes of the Niam-Niam and Monbuttu, who, by the physical development of the race, as well as by the branches of industry and arts which they cultivate, appear so manifestly of a superior order that they have been supposed to be related to the Fellatas of the west.

The second of the two great groups of native tribes of Central Africa consists of the Bantoo negroes. They belong to the Caffre race, the characteristics of which are reproduced in them, but not without numerous deviations and shades. Generally, these negroes have a clearer complexion than those of the Soudan; the combined expression of the characteristic traits of these last exhibits a sensible degree of enfeeblement. Except on the east coast, near Zanzibar, they have remained absolutely rebels against Mohammedanism, so that their primitive institutions have not been changed thereby. The splitting up of these tribes is extreme; the number of communities thus formed is as considerable as their composition is changeable. The family has continued to form the basis of their political organisation; they have rarely risen above the state of life of a tribe. The authority of the chiefs is confined to certain villages, and although frequently arbitrary and cruel, is scarcely so despotic as in the Mussulman States. The laws of succession are uncertain; the groupings of families very shifting. English travellers, however, who almost exclusively have explored these regions, Livingstone and Cameron in particular, have made us acquainted with some important states of the centre of Africa. Such are the empires of Muata-Yamvo, east of the Portuguese Government of Angola; of Casembe, south-west of Lake Tanganyika; of the Makololo on the Upper Zambesi; of the Matebele on the right bank of the same river, etc. More northward, the expeditions directed towards the sources of the Nile have revealed the existence of a whole series of states spread along the borders of the great lakes; those of Karagwe, of Kittara, and of Uganda with its king, Mtesa, from their well-known tendencies, only wait for the establishment of a regular line of communication with the coast, to enter on the broad roads of civilisation.

The classification of the negroes, in the religious point of view, corresponds tolerably exactly with their ethnographical division. An oblique line drawn from the mouth of the Senegal to Zanzibar defines the two great forms of creed. All north of that line, with the exception of Abyssinia and the negro tribes of the Upper Nile, belongs to Mohammedanism: in the south, fetishism and idolatry prevail. The worship of the shades of the dead, or of ancestors, exists amongst numerous tribes, and gives rise to frequent human sacrifices. The belief in magic, sorcery, and talismans, is diffused everywhere, and is the cause of many calamities. The brutality of fetishism and the sufferings which it leads to are active aids to the propagation of Mohammedanism: but this itself is only an improvement half-way. The polygamy, slavery, and despotism which it introduces in its train, can only bring with them a low degree of civilisation.

With the exception of the principalities of the Soudan, the political and social institutions of the negroes have continued in a state of infancy, but judicial institutions are better developed. Among many communities a remarkable judicial instinct exists; suits are well followed up, and the parties exhibit no lack of telling arguments. Three degrees of proceeding are observed: the superior court consists of the old men, who give judgment according to established rule. If precedents are wanting, a consultation is held among the tribes. Calumny is put down as on a level with robbery; the producing of abortion is regarded as a crime.

Among all the negroes the well-being of the family

suffers from polygamy and slavery; this double scourge is universal. Filial affection is strongly developed, but it extends almost exclusively to the mother. The Damaras swear "by the tears of their mother." The negro females justify this devotion by the maternal attentions which they lavish on their offspring. Domestic life wears a character of great simplicity; its necessities are very limited. A taste for dress exists and is often exhibited in the most grotesque disguises, but for the most part, except in the states of the Soudan, the costume is limited to the most indispensable garments; the state of simple nature is not uncommon. The predominant character of the negro is that of a big child. He is artless, free from care, lazy, full of fun, fond of festivities, of music, and of dancing. Kindliness is natural to him, but intercourse with the slave merchants make him mistrustful, and sometimes cruel. One characteristic is to be noticed: viz., the existence, in different degrees, of cannibalism among many of the tribes, and, by a strange contradiction, these are generally the handsomest in form and the most advanced in civilisation.

Agriculture and the breeding of cattle are the two principal branches of industry among the negroes; the former prevails in the states of the Soudan, the latter in Central Africa. The wealth of cereals and of cattle is very great, the produce being susceptible of an almost unlimited development. Many growths, such as those of the doucq and the ground-nut (*Arachis hypogæa*) seem to be indigenous; those of maize, of manioc, of wheat and barley, are spread throughout the whole of Equatorial Africa, but have been introduced from outside. It is noteworthy that the negroes everywhere use milk and its derivatives.

Among the industrial arts cultivated by the tribes of the interior of Africa, pottery, exhibiting both skill and taste, holds the first place. All, from the inhabitants of Kordofan down to the Hottentots, are acquainted with the art of casting iron and copper; they draw off a very pure metal, of which they make both utensils and arms. In Bornou, they have attained the art of casting cannon; at several places they make guns, helmets, and coats of mail. The Ashantees work in gold and have skilful goldsmiths. The tanning of hides, the weaving of mats, the art of sewing, of weaving and dyeing cotton are widely spread among the negroes, and many of their productions are remarkable for the solidity as well as the fineness of the work. These results of a growing spirit of industry deserve the attention of Europe. The negro in himself has but little invention, but he possesses in a high degree the desire and the ability to learn; he easily lays hold of the information which is brought within his reach, and, in order to raise the level of his moral and social standard at once and to a considerable elevation, all that is wanted is the organisation of a practical mode of instructing him in the arts and handicrafts of Europe.

Commerce exists under primitive forms in all the countries of Central Africa. Every village has a market, and the towns have several. Goods are paid for in kind or with money. In the Northern States dollars of the coin of Maria Theresa, gold-dust, cowries (the African small coin) are the principal mediums of exchange. The commerce of the interior, of which the necessaries of life form the basis, is tolerably active.

The export is confined to a small number of articles, principally ivory, ostrich feathers, gums, etc. The most important of all, however, is *man* himself. Here comes in the question of the slave trade, and this grave subject deserves the most serious attention, for it is the opinion of all travellers and missionaries that it exercises a preponderating influence over the moral and social condition of the races of Central Africa, and it will not do to dream of civilising them until an end has been put to what Livingstone justly called the MONSTER INIQUITY.

CHAPTER IV.

THE AFRICAN SLAVE TRADE OF THE NINETEENTH CENTURY—TERRITORIES OVER WHICH IT EXTENDS—CHARACTER AND IMPORTANCE OF ITS OPERATIONS.

Not one of the least strange among the phenomena of this age of publicity, is the almost universal ignorance and even indifference which prevail in our midst with regard to the African Slave Trade. If, however, there be a subject which appeals in a high degree to the pity as well as the justice of Europe, it is this. On a continent, in immediate and continuous contact with our own, at our very doors and under our eyes, a system of brigandage, of devastation and massacres, the daily horrors of which are scarcely equalled by the most sanguinary wars recorded at wide intervals in history, has been organised and prospers. Since the abolition of slavery in America, since the official proscription of the slave trade by all civilised nations, it would seem that man-hunting ought naturally to have disappeared, or at least have been reduced to insignificant proportions. Nothing of the sort. The traffic in slaves exists, and has its regular markets of supply and of sale, and the number of its victims is reckoned every year by hundreds of thousands. Let us for a moment take a close view of this abominable trade. Its details are revealed to us by English Parliamentary documents and by African travellers, and have been taken up with equal knowledge and feeling by M. Berlioux in his work on 'La Traite Orientale.'*

Man-hunting is organised in three great regions of Africa: the states of the Soudan, the Valley of the Upper Nile, and the central plateau. On the west coast the cruisers have nearly put an end to this odious traffic.

In the Soudan, the providers of the slave dealers are no other than the native princes themselves. It is the principal source of their revenues. As disciples of

* Paris, 1870. Also may be consulted with advantage: J. Cooper, 'The Lost Continent.' London, 1875.

Islam, they look upon the Pagan populations, whether subject to their own states or not, as devoid of every kind of right in the presence of believers; the raids which they organise, and in which they interest the leaders and soldiers of their little armies, extend over vast territories. They surround and set fire to villages, they kill everything which resists or appears unsuited for marching, for labour, or for pleasure; the rest they take away. The devastation and carnage which mark the track of these sinister expeditions are indescribable; whole provinces which had recently been populous and prosperous are sometimes found, after the lapse of a few years, deserted and waste.

The produce of these raids are taken to the markets of the interior; Kuka in Bornou is one of the principal. "The purchasers of Kuka," writes M. Berlioux, "understand their business. The traffic is accordingly exhibited in all its melancholy hideousness. The slaves are filthy and covered with wretched rags; they are examined; their size is measured; the mouth is opened to see the teeth, and inquiries are made whether they eat well, because the appetite is looked upon as a sign of health. A young boy fetches from fifteen to thirty dollars (the thaler is worth three shillings); a young girl sells for from thirty to sixty dollars; the young Fellata girls, whose complexion is clear and features regular, always fetch more. An old man or matron goes at a price of from three to ten dollars. This is also the price of a child. On Monday, the market day, it often happens that thousands of slaves are put up for sale; every other day, one is sure to find small clusters of some hundreds. Thus every week there are brought into the market-place at Kuka at least five or six thousand slaves."

A portion of these unfortunates remain in the country for the necessities of the interior: the great mass of them are bought by Arab merchants and marched across the desert under a burning sun, by arid roads from seven to nine hundred miles in length to Murzook, the capital of Fezzan, a tributary province of Turkey. The privations and tortures that these troops of slaves— the great annual caravan from Kuka alone conveys about 4000—suffer is inconceivable. "On both sides of the road," says G. Rohlfs, "are seen the blanched bones of dead slaves; some skeletons still have on them the katoun (garment) of the negroes. Even a person who is ignorant of the road from Bornou has only to follow the bones which lie scattered right and left of the road, and he will make no mistake."

The slave trade to Fezzan is reckoned at 10,000 head per annum; one dealer alone had imported in one year (1864) 1100. This human cattle is brought in at night, with the complicity of the Turkish agents, who receive a premium of ten francs per slave. From Murzook, the caravans journey eastwards to Cairo, where they discharge their merchandise. Some idea may be formed of the extent of the evil caused by the slave trade in the Soudan, when one reflects that it carries off annually about 15,000 men, that it destroys at least an equal number, that it spreads insecurity and unceasing alarms among a number of tribes, and condemns to sterility provinces of incomparable richness.

The second theatre of the slave trade is met with in the Valley of the Upper Nile, among the very little advanced negro tribes of the Shilluks, the Dinkas, the Djurs, etc. Its controllers are partly Egyptian and Arab merchants, and partly adventurers from all countries, the scum of the nations of Europe. It is the ivory trade which has been the point of departure of the slave trade, and which serves as a cloak to it at the present time. The dealers select for themselves a field of operation, sometimes as extensive as a province. In the middle is constructed an entrenched camp, inhabited by the speculator or his deputy, the servants and the hunters and soldiers, the number of which varies from 100 to 300; this is called a Seribah. At the commencement, the allotted task of these men was to hunt elephants; a primitive mode of making a fortune which has long since been abandoned. It has been found more profitable first to buy of the negroes the ivory they had to dispose of, and afterwards to take it from them; once arrived at that point, they completed the operation by carrying off their cattle, and finally, the people themselves. More than twenty years ago, man-hunting was established in these countries on the same footing as in the Soudan, and an idea may be formed of its activity from the fact that, in 1864, one single *battue* led to the capture of 8000 slaves.

The head-quarters of the slave trade is established at Khartoom, under the too unobservant eyes of the Egyptian authorities. From this point the greater number of the slaves are sent to Massowa, whence they are taken to the markets of the East. They reach Khartoom by the affluents of the Nile, packed in chains, like cattle, in boats which are the ordinary abodes of the smallpox and the plague.

There are twenty Seribahs on the Upper Nile. The average profit of each master is reckoned by Sir Samuel Baker at 450 slaves per annum; the soldiers and hunters receive their pay in slaves. These facts show an annual total of at least 20,000 head. If to these be added the men taken in the raids, the number of negroes carried off every year by the trade in the valley of the Upper Nile cannot be reckoned at less than 30,000, without including those that are left on the field of battle or on the road.

The central plateau of Africa is the third theatre on which this execrable traffic is carried on, and nowhere has it produced more cruel ravages. Scarcely has the traveller passed the boundaries of the sultanate of Zanzibar, than he comes upon the regions of Usagara, and Ugongo, formerly called the garden of Africa, but now uncultivated and waste under the influence of the slave trade. The inhabitants scattered in the woods watch with an hostile eye the passage of the traveller and of the caravans. Throughout the whole of this eastern zone the slave trade has assumed the appearance of a war of races: it is the contest of the Arab invader against the native negro, the former armed with gun and revolver, the latter having no arms to defend himself with but the javelin and the arrow. The expeditions penetrate to great distances into the interior; they reach beyond the Tanganyika as far as the kingdom of Cazembe. At some points the Arab traders have discovered the art of associating in their infernal operations their very victims themselves. The hunting then becomes complicated with a multitude of intestine wars between the tribes, which prove more fruitful for the spoilers, and still more disastrous for the natives. Under the influence of these degrading alliances, negroes have been known to sell themselves to negroes, and to deliver up their own children into slavery.

It is at Kaseh or Taboro, some hundred leagues from the eastern shore of the Tanganyika that the headquarters of the Arab dealers are located. " Here, from the plateau to the sea, from the point where the raid has taken place, to the port of embarkation, the journey is no longer reckoned by tedious weeks, and it can be made with smaller numbers. But it is requisite to go fast, for behind the rocks or in the depth of the copses ambuscades may lie concealed. The native does not spare the Arab, when he finds a favourable opportunity. "Walk quickly," is the repeated order to the shackled slaves; but when the order is no more heard, and the stick has no more effect on the wretch overdone with fatigue, he is pitilessly left in the midst of the solitude. Baker tells us of a convoy brought back not by Arabs but by Turks. The old women carried off in the raid were not proceeding fast enough. So soon as fatigue caused one to fall, she was felled; a blow of a club on the neck, and a carcase only remained in the throes of death. The road was dotted with these frightful beacons. On approaching the sea, when the danger seems past, then the interest of the dealer suggests somewhat more precaution. If in the troop there remain some men to whom hunger and fatigue have left a little strength, they are made to carry their enfeebled companions. There is something horrible and sickening in such a caravan. The troop no longer proceeds in a body; the unfortunates are clustered in groups along the road, stumbling about and like so many skeletons: their countenances no longer bearing any expression but that of famine, their eyes wan and sunken, and their cheeks bony. But what benefit will this close of their journey bring to the poor wretches? The black boats are there, sombre, narrow, fetid, waiting for the human merchandise. Here we have the slave trade in all its physical hideousness. It would be more frightful still if it were possible to expose before our eyes the moral sores, the vices, the revolting degradation which slavery produces both in the master and in the slave." *

This lamentable and sickening picture is by no means

* Berlioux, 'La Traite Orientale,' p. 248.

borrowed from the imagination. It is strictly confirmed in all its details by the narratives of travellers. It is repeated every year from the eastern side of the African plateau, over an extent of 600,000 square miles, from the top of Tanganyika to the extremity of Lake Nyassa. It is in fact on the shores of this latter lake that the trade is most active and the most disastrous in its effects. In 1851 Livingstone visited this previously unknown country. He found there a numerous population, devoted to agricultural labour and initiated in the primitive arts of civilisation. The climate appeared to him so beautiful, the land so fruitful, the men so kindly, that he conceived the idea of founding a colony in those parts. Ten years later, in 1861 and 1863, the illustrious traveller again visited the same places. He no longer recognised them; the slave trade had reached there in the interval. The plantations had disappeared; the villages were burnt; the inhabitants dispersed, carried off or killed. The copses were filled with bloody corpses; the rivers were choked with them; from the branches of the trees hung women whom the chief of the band had condemned to perish when exhaustion prevented their following the convoy any longer, by way of intimidating their companions, or of revenge for the losses sustained. Livingstone, whose noble and heroic figure appears at every point of this immense field of carnage as the representative of justice and the vindicator of the rights of humanity, denounces these and such like scenes at every step: the disgust and horror occasioned by them poisoned the closing days of his life. "When I have endeavoured," he wrote a short time before his death, "to give some idea of the slave trade and its attendant evils in this country, it was necessary to keep far within the truth in order not to be thought guilty of exaggeration. But, in sober seriousness, the subject does not admit of being over-drawn. To exaggerate its enormities is a simple impossibility. The sights I have seen, though common incidents of the so-called trade, are so terribly nauseous, that I always strive to drive them from memory; and in cases of other disagreeable recollections, I can, in time, succeed in consigning them to oblivion. These slaving scenes, however, come back unbidden and unwelcome, and sometimes make me start up at dead of night, horrified by their vividness."

The evil must indeed be very great when we see the results which it produces. Colonel Rigby, the English Consul at Zanzibar, reckons at 19,000 the number of negroes which the Nyassa country supplies annually to that place. The port of Quiloa serves here as the base of operations for the traffic in slaves. When we combine this export movement with that which exists on both sides of the Tanganyika, we arrive at a total of not less than 40,000 captives carried off every year on the west coast of Africa. Since the interdiction by recent treaties of the exportation of slaves by Zanzibar, the effect has been that the trade has been carried further north, and the expeditions from Muscat and Quiloa defy the efforts of the English cruisers.

The figures just quoted, although taken at the lowest estimate, need no commentary. They show between 80,000 and 90,000 as the number of negroes annually taken by force from Africa. This amount is equivalent to the losses of a great war; and what renders it the more frightful is that in itself it is but a fraction of a total to be taken into account in far other senses. Livingstone declares that the number of slaves which reach the coast only represents the fifth part, and in certain districts even, where the resistance is more energetic, the tenth part of the real victims of the trade. The others die in the attacks on the villages and in the massacres and conflagrations which accompany them, or else perish along the roads during the march of the convoys or on board the boats. The destruction of human life would thus reach annually to 400,000 persons at least. According to Sir Bartle Frere, this minimum is far exceeded. The superior of the Catholic mission of Central Africa estimates at a million of men the amount of loss which the slave trade inflicts annually on the populations of Africa. These estimates cease to cause astonishment when we reflect that the trade rages over a territory as extensive as the whole of Europe, inhabited by about eighty millions of negroes.

Whither flows this unceasingly renewed stream of slaves?

After the suppression of all the colonial markets, there

scarcely remain any but those of the East. Egypt, Arabia, Turkey, both European and Asiatic, Persia and Madagascar, these are henceforth the countries of destination for this human merchandise. Far from diminishing, the demand only increases; the fresh outbreak, for instance, of slavery in Egypt, is a certain fact. It would seem that in proportion as their own vitality dies out, Mussulman communities experience a greater need of foreign strength. The negro, moreover, does not breed in the countries of the East: the second generation is rare; the third does not exist. When to this is added the horrible practice of castration, kept up in Turkey and Egypt, which kills two out of three of the wretched children subjected to this torture, it will be understood how this demand for African blood remains constantly fresh, and constantly pressing.

It is high time that civilised nations should combine in one generous and powerful effort to put an end to such abominable iniquities. Without the absolute suppression of the slave trade, every attempt at introducing civilisation into Africa, must, at best, be fruitless. This has been the rock on which past enterprises have split, this is still the stumbling-block of new establishments. By setting up in perpetuity a foreign and a civil warfare in the heart of Africa, the slave trade stifles therein every germ of progress, and unceasingly replunges into barbarism the communities which were beginning to extricate themselves from it. The profits of the odious traffic are moreover so enormous that they prevent the establishment of all legitimate commerce: honest merchants could not find a channel for their products, and the natives have no interest in increasing their own, while the foreigner nearly everywhere runs the risk of being taken for an enemy. Such is the work of the slave trade, and here we see the reason why Africa has remained for four centuries stationary, and, except at a few points in her seaboard, has not made a step in the way of civilisation.

SECOND PART.

THE BRUSSELS GEOGRAPHICAL CONFERENCE.

SECOND PART.

THE BRUSSELS GEOGRAPHICAL CONFERENCE.

CHAPTER V.

THE BRUSSELS GEOGRAPHICAL CONFERENCE — ITS PROGRAMME AND OBJECT—INTERNATIONAL STATIONS IN AFRICA.

However contracted may be the frame of the foregoing picture, and soberly as we have been obliged to handle its details, it nevertheless justifies in its general features the three following conclusions, which it is of importance to place in a clear light:

1. Africa, in its extension across three zones, presents, thanks to the relief of its surface and the distribution of its waters, the most various conditions of habitability. It is not absolutely impenetrable at any point; it is rich in products of every kind, and possesses in abundance all the resources which form the material basis of civilisation.

2. The African populations, both the Berbers of the north and the negroes of the centre and of the south, are neither unfitted for nor opposed to all improvement. Christianity, science, and commerce are capable of changing their whole social condition. The phenomenon which has been produced in America will certainly not be repeated in Africa. The negroes will not disappear, like the Indians, from the contact with a superior civilisation; they will rather be enticed by it. The advances which they have already realised under the least favorable circumstances are a guarantee for the future. Doubtless no one could fix the limit to which education will be able to lead them, but it is a demonstrated fact that that education is possible.*

3. If, for four centuries, Europe's acquaintance with Africa and the condition of its inhabitants has been at a standstill, the principal, if not the only, cause has

---

* Peschel, in his 'Treatise on Ethnography,' quotes this indication of genius in a Vei negro, who succeeded in reducing the idiom spoken by his fellow citizens into a distinct alphabet. He had been, it is true, educated by Europeans; but this circumstance precisely shows to what a point the negro is capable of receiving and utilising instruction.

been the existence of the slave trade. The slave trade is the enemy and the stumbling-block of all progress. It exists and it spreads, even in our own days, in spite of the formal proscription levelled at it, time after time, by all civilised nations. The period is now come for giving an effective and universal support both to their declarations and their engagements. Every attempt to civilise the populations of Africa must have for its immediate object the extinction of the trade, not only in its direct manifestations but also in the principle which feeds it, viz., the institution of slavery itself both in the Mussulman States in the east and among Africans themselves.

These three fundamental truths explain the whole work of the Conference, for they have been the point of departure and the rule of its labours. The possibility of "definitively planting the standard of civilisation on the soil of Central Africa"—these are the very words of the Royal opening address*—was never for an instant placed in doubt. The discussion was directly brought to bear upon the practical means of carrying it out,

---

* See the text of this document in Appendix II.

and with regard to this, the Conference has had to examine in its turn what it was advisable to do in Africa and what it was possible to propose to Europe.

The creation of a system of permanent stations distributed over different points of the African Continent was the first of these means which the Conference had to consider. In proposing the establishment of them, the King of the Belgians described at the same time in his address, their triple character: they were to be at once stations for the relief of travellers, for the advancement of science, and for the promotion of peace. This combination did not give rise to the least objection. The celebrated travellers who were present at the meeting at Brussels were unanimous in declaring that the existence of such establishments would render invaluable services to their successors, and would effectively promote the work of scientific exploration. One amongst them, M. Rohlfs, even remarked that the English had already founded, under the form of religious missions or diplomatic posts, some establishments of the same kind, though, it is true, on a much more modest scale than might be expected from an international association. Difficulties, doubtless, of more than one kind were foreseen, but no one looked upon them as insurmountable.

What will be the duties that these stations will have to fulfil? They will be of a triple character, corresponding to the several objects which the Conference proposed to itself when it decided on establishing them.

But before entering on this subject, an explanation is necessary. The Conference of Brussels took no measures towards its own organisation of scientific expeditions, but it did not preclude itself from the employment of its exertions in this direction. If its resources became developed, and if the solution of any problem appeared essential to its objects, it would certainly be able, without deviating from its programme, to afford relief to travellers or even to send out such at its own expense. This task, which, moreover, must, it would seem, be an exceptional one, depends upon the contingencies of the future; under present circumstances, the Conference has had to leave it in the hands of governments, of geographical societies, and, above all, to private initiation, which, hitherto, has appeared to be the most successful and the most profitable. In fact, experience has shown that national expeditions provided with a numerous retinue and a great train of baggage, scarcely ever succeed; the army of porters which they require, the difficulty of provisioning them and of maintaining order and discipline, are rocks on which all run aground. The most remarkable discoveries, the most daring campaigns, have, on the contrary, been the work of isolated travellers. It is true that, in their case, obstacles and dangers are not wanting either, and the results are often incomplete: insufficiency of supplies, or exhaustion of strength will often necessitate an interruption to explorations in the full tide of success; but it is precisely at this point that the international association proposes to step in. By tracing a united plan of investigation, it organises system between individual enterprises, introduces therein unity and combination, and prevents the loss of time and strength. By establishing stations in the interior of Africa, it supports the traveller in his journey, gives him greater security, and enables him to bring to bear directly upon his object all the energy and endurance which he possesses.

The permanent stations which will be established on the soil of Africa, will be, then, pre-eminently relief stations.

They will neither be the object nor the terminus of new expeditions; they do not precede exploration, they follow it. Established at first on the seaboard, they will advance progressively towards the interior, securing behind them, as far as may be feasible, regular communications with the coast. In this manner, bases of operations will be formed, which, when united, will become lines, and finally roads. For the most part, travellers will start from the stations to penetrate into the heart of the country. The stations will serve as a protection to them, to lend security and brightness to their journey, as a storehouse for completing or renewing their provisions, their means of study or exchange, as an infirmary in case of sickness, and as a refuge on which they can fall back in case of danger. The destitution and privations, the physical and moral sufferings which have so severely tried the

Livingstones, the Rohlfs, the Nachtigals, the Schweinfurths and the Camerons, and so often forced them to renounce the extension of their discoveries, will be less to be feared. In the stations, travellers will become the guests of Europe; there they will be able to take rest from their fatigues, and await the propitious moment for resuming their journey; their powers of resistance and perseverance will be in a great measure increased, and the final end of their labours will be brought sensibly nearer.

But while the principal object of the stations is to afford relief, it is by no means confined to that duty; it is also scientific. Each post will naturally become a centre of studies and researches of every kind: on the character and aspect of the soil, the products, the climate, the surrounding populations, their wants, their resources, etc. The traveller traces his line in the unknown: the station radiates within a limited diameter, no doubt, but exhausting all the better the circle over which it presides. It will be at the same time, a little observatory and a museum, in which will be accumulated the observations and collections which would be made, primarily, in the service of science, and secondarily, for the advancement of commerce, industry, and civilisation.

To meet these manifold requirements the stations should be supplied with a tolerable variety of utensils, and be provided with stores of every kind. It is not sufficient for them to have enough for their own needs: they will have to provide for those of the travellers whom they will be bound to re-victual. To the character of relief station and scientific observatory will further be added that of a depôt, or warehouse, containing such articles as are most indispensable for African travellers; maps and special books; astronomical and scientific instruments, medicines, and clothes, merchandise, and funds, etc.

To aid science then, and the men who constitute themselves her apostles, will be the immediate and essential object of the stations which are about to be established in Africa. In a short time another not less important one will be added thereto, viz.:—that of diffusing the light of civilisation among the natives. The Conference has not discussed or arranged the details of all these questions; it has reserved this task for the central committee of management, which it appointed before closing its labours; but its general intention in this direction has been very clearly defined. It was formulated with *éclat* by the king, on opening the first session of the assembly, which, on its part, has invariably continued to entertain the same view. The stations then will be all equally mediums of civilisation, means of promoting progress, and guarantees of peace for the populations amongst which they will be established. From this point of view, the duties of these establishments extend over a wide area, and take a considerable range.

It would doubtless be overstepping the intention, and overloading the already very complicated duties, of the stations, to aim at the immediate initiation of the negroes into the arts of civilisation. They cannot be, in the strict sense of the word, professional schools, or apprentices' workshops; but, by the fact alone of their presence, and the daily practice of simple arts, under the eyes of the natives, by the contrast of European existence, of its manners, customs, and modes of working, with the rudeness of savage life, there will be established a medium of real instruction, and a practical education, the results of which cannot fail to be important. Little by little, by the irresistible attraction which knowledge exercises over ignorance, and strength over weakness, new populations will settle around the stations, and, under their influence, will assume the aspect of better organised communities. The dissensions and quarrels so frequent among the tribes, and so fatal to individual liberty may thus be extinguished or suppressed. By his influence, and by the services which he will be called upon to render them, the governor of the station will insensibly become an arbiter, who will promote peace and harmony among them. This duty will lead to another of still greater utility to the interests of civilisation. If the European stations should, as will certainly be attempted, be ranged, from preference, along the regular highway of the slave trade, they will be able to organise effective plans in opposition to it, for the defence of the natives, and for barring the road against the convoys of slaves. The difficulty will not be so great as might be thought at first sight. It will nearly always be sufficient to provide Africans with fire-arms, to destroy the one only superiority which the kidnappers possess over the negroes, whom now they make their victims. The cowardice of kidnappers, is, by the testimony of all travellers, equal to their cruelty: it will not need a very great exertion of strength to keep them at a distance.

Here arises a series of questions, each one more serious and complex than the other. Will the stations be occupied by a numerous and armed staff? Will they be of a national, international, or compound character? Is their organisation to be strictly circumscribed within the limits of civilisation and science; or is it to be further developed in a religious and commercial direction? The solution of the greater part of these questions is reserved for the future; the Conference has not made it the subject of a special debate; its intention, however, has been manifested too clearly to admit of any doubt as to the essential bases of the undertaking.

For example: the stations will have no military

surroundings; they will be established under conditions as simple and inexpensive as possible. Sir Bartle Frere has well defined their principle of action; under all circumstances they will have recourse to gentleness persuasion, and that natural ascendancy which emanates from the superiority of civilised man. Hence the numerical strength will scarcely need to be very great. A chief who must be at the same time a man of action and a man of science either theoretical or technical, a medical naturalist, perhaps a physical astronomer, five or six artisans, skilled in various handicrafts, will probably in most cases suffice. The number of persons will rarely exceed, under ordinary conditions, ten or twelve men; in certain respects a newly established station may even fall below this figure.

As for the second problem, the international point of view has been that which has influenced the Conference; but it has evidently not been its intention to exclude or oppose any generous proposition.

The same feeling has influenced the Conference in the solution of the third question. Sir H. Rawlinson and Vice-Admiral de la Roncière-le-Noury, have given expression to very just views on this point, which corresponded with the opinions held by the Conference. "We must not," said the former, "give the stations an exclusively religious, political, or commercial character; they should be centres of information, medical assistance, and civilisation. "Religious missions," added the second, "which need not be immediately organised, but which might follow the establishment of stations, would be a useful medium of co-operation. Commercial relations, which it is a matter of general interest to form and extend, conduce to the same result." From the tenor of these expressions, the establishments which it is proposed to form, will bear a purely lay character; the international assembly bore no other; they impose upon themselves no religious mission, they represent no creed, no form of worship.

This abstention, however, proceeds neither from indifference nor scepticism. Far from being hostile to the preaching of the gospel, the greater part of the members of the Conference were of opinion that this preaching would be highly salutary, and might become the most active forerunner of the moral regeneration of the nations of Africa. History shows that Christianity possesses a special virtue for rescuing savage races from barbarism, and making them rapidly overstep the first barriers to civilisation. This great and legitimate influence will not therefore be disregarded, but its guidance must necessarily rest in the hands of the Christian Churches. The isolated efforts of propagandism, made up to these later times, at different points of Africa, have given but unsatisfactory results; they might be resumed under more favourable conditions. Missionaries will be free to come and establish themselves in the neighbourhood of the stations, and to erect, within their range, places of worship and schools: to whatever creed they belong, they will receive from them aid and support; they will avail themselves of the relations which may have been established and the advances already gained, and will be able effectively to contribute to their consolidation and extension.

This principle is of general application. While

limiting the field of their own efforts, in order to render them more effective, the stations do not exclude other forms of action; they rather encourage them and support them with their patronage. By the same process, the question of economical relationships is solved. International establishments could not be counting-houses, any more than they could be missions; yet, so far has the Conference been from disregarding the importance of the commercial question, that one of its most distinguished members, Dr. Nachtigal, felt justified in saying that: "It is by commerce that the interior of Africa will best be civilised." The spirit of enterprise will therefore be able to give itself scope; and the stations, without relinquishing their special task, will actively support that spirit; while it, in its turn, will become a powerful auxiliary to them.

These considerations recall to us one of the most remarkable pages of the 'Géographie comparée' of Carl Ritter; that learned geographer applied the remark only to the Soudan, but later discoveries have proved it to be of general application. "Commerce," he says, "opens all roads in Africa, and civilisation can make no way but in its train. The enfeeblement of the domination of the Moors in the negro states, on the banks of the Niger, offers now, to Europeans and Christianity, a favourable opportunity for entering the Soudan. The agents of the powers and of European commercial houses, might establish themselves much more easily there than in the Mohammedan East. The English residents accredited to the courts of the north and of the south, to Murzook, in the Fezzan, and to Coomassie in the country of Ashantee, the colonies of the Senegal and of the Gambia, and, above all, the fair and flourishing state of Sierra Leone, are already, if we were only wise enough to take advantage of them, the most important stepping-stones for arriving at the realisation of this idea. A direct commerce of Europeans with the markets of the Soudan, such as Mungo Park and his successors endeavoured to introduce on the banks of the Gambia, would give more political independence to the negro states, and more prosperity to individuals, and would render them independent of the Moors and Arabs. By this means they might be supplied with fire-arms for self-defence, and missionaries would have an opportunity of converting and civilising them as at Sierra Leone. One result of these generous efforts would be the complete and progressive abolition of the slave trade, from the interior to the coasts. But, in the first place, it would be necessary to substitute for it another traffic equally advantageous to the native princes, whose principal revenues are derived from slave-hunting and from tributes paid in slaves. Commerce with Europeans would soon afford them profits, both safer and larger. By this means, the Mohammedans would be deprived of the pretext for slave-hunting. For, according to the Koran, they consider it their duty to make war on idolaters, and their right to throw heathens into slavery and bondage. These enterprises would favour and powerfully help the emancipation of the negroes of the Soudan, which, meanwhile, can only be the result of their own exertions, for experience has proved that it cannot be effected by maritime operations, not even if thousands of generous individuals were to unite their subscriptions and their efforts; not even if all the nations of Christianity were to combine in the resolution."*

The principle, the character, and the work of the African stations being well defined, where will it be convenient, in the first instance, to establish them? The examination of this important question occupied the whole of the second session of the Conference. Two projects were presented for consideration; the first, by General Sir H. Rawlinson in the name of the English, French, and Italian members of the Conference, especially directed attention to the final object to be attained; the second, formulated by M. de Semenow in the name of the German, Austrian, and Russian members, took more into consideration the conditions of the point of departure. The Belgian members refrained from opposing a third project to the two others, in order to leave the initiative, in pursuance of the declaration made by the king, "exclusively to the representatives of states, whose authority in this

* Ritter, 'Géographie générale comparée,' translated by E. Bervet and E. Desor, p. 258. Brussels, 1837.

matter is founded upon long experience and brilliant services."

The report drawn up by Sir H. Rawlinson, without neglecting the interests of science, had a strong economical and political bearing; it proposed a continuous line of communication to be established between the east and west coasts of Africa to the south of the equator. This line would debouch on the east, in the neighbourhood of Zanzibar; on the west, at St. Paul de Loanda; stations, or at least agencies, should be posted along its extent. Two localities were fixed upon for the present; Ujiji, on Lake Tanganyika, and Nyangwe, on the upper course of the Lualaba. From the main trunk should be sent out three subsidiary branches, the first in the direction of the mouth of the Congo, the second towards the sources of the Nile, and the third to strike the Zambezi. These two last branches would, when united, form a grand continuous line, crossing the first, and extending from the Valley of the Nile on the north, to that of the Zambezi on the south, across the great lakes. Steam-boats launched on the Victoria, the Tanganyika, and the Nyassa would unite the land sections of the route. It was a grand conception, exhibiting the genius and the spirit of enterprise peculiar to powerful maritime nations. It may have taken too little into account the difficulties of a first attempt; this defect does not interfere with its conformity with the several objects contemplated by the Conference, nor with its continuing to be the programme for the future, should circumstances prove favourable to the undertaking.

The report presented by M. de Semenow, was conceived on less extensive bases; the interests of science alone had evidently influenced the group to whose ideas this report gave expression. It proposed to organise, upon a combined plan, the exploration of the as yet unknown regions of Central Africa, confiding this task to individual travellers starting from opposite points and relying on relief-stations. These stations should be established simultaneously on the coast, at Bagamoyo (near Zanzibar), and at Loanda, for instance, as well as in the interior, following as well as might be the track of Cameron; the points of Ujiji,

Nyangwe, etc., were indicated. With respect to the junction of these stations by regular roads of communication, it was doubted whether this plan would be at present practicable: it was a result to be looked for from the future development of the undertaking. This project exhibited more limited views than those expressed in the report of General Rawlinson, but it was more practical; it was founded on recent experience, and while concentrating the first efforts of the Conference on scientific exploration, did not exclude more remote anticipations nor more complicated enterprises.

The system which has been preferred is one of compromise. Its formula has been determined by a mixed committee, of which the learned secretary-general of the Society of Geography of Paris, M. Maunoir, is the reporter. This document constitutes the official declaration of the Conference with reference to the mission undertaken by the international association created under its auspices. Its immediate object is appointed to be the exploration of the as yet unknown parts of Equatorial Africa. Individual travellers will be the active instruments, and the stations will be the relief posts of this exploration. These latter will be established at first on the seaboard, viz., at Bagamoyo, in the Sultan of Zanzibar's territories, on the Indian Ocean side, and at St. Paul de Loanda, in the Portuguese possessions on the Atlantic side. Other stations will be placed in the interior: at Ujiji, on the eastern shore of Lake Tanganyika; at Nyangwe, on the Lualaba, at some hundred leagues from the western shore of the same lake, the extreme point reached to the northward by Livingstone and Cameron; and at a spot to be determined on hereafter, in the states of the principal chief of Central Africa, Muata-Yamvo. These posts describe on the map, to the south of the equator, an oblique line stretching from north-east to south-west, which corresponds exactly, except at the western point of abutment, with the route of Captain Cameron. The Conference, thus reproducing under a modified form the suggestion of the Anglo-Italian-French group, concludes by expressing the wish that the stations may be connected by a line of communication, "as far as possible continuous," and that the lines perpendicular to the first may be opened in the direction of from north to south.

Such are, in substance, the declaration of the Conference, and the suggestions from which that declaration proceeds. This manifestly opens up an immense career both to science and to civilisation; it will produce glorious and fruitful results, if all the forces mustered to carry it into actual operation are deeply imbued with the sense of their noble mission, and acquit themselves of it with unflagging zeal.

CHAPTER VI.

ORGANISATION OF THE INTERNATIONAL ASSOCIATION FOR THE EXPLORATION AND CIVILISATION OF AFRICA—DUTIES AND RELATIONS OF THE COMMITTEES.

IF an institution is to live and prosper, it is not merely requisite that it should have a well-traced programme and a definite object, it must also have an organisation suited to its nature, which will enable it to come forward and act, uniting as in a sheaf the forces at its disposal, and importing into its action, consecutiveness, harmony, and unity. This essential point has not escaped the attention of the Conference; it has been the subject of its latest consultations. It has been concluded that travellers and stations are to be regarded as the representatives and agents of the association on the soil of Africa; the former will be the auxiliaries, the latter the instruments of its scientific and humanitarian intentions. But in the old as in the new continent, it was necessary to create a system of organisation conceived on an entirely different footing, in consequence of its having an entirely different mission. The Conference has had to find within its own compass the plan and the first elements of this system.

Seven nations, being no other than the six great European powers and Belgium, have had their delegates at the Conference of Brussels. Unforeseen circumstances, overruling accidents, have caused some of these delegations to be incomplete, but in no way modifying the good intention. No sort of public mandate was connected with their functions; all the members of the assembly have acted and spoken in their own names; but they had been selected in such a manner as that they should faithfully represent, whether they were one or many, the opinion of their different nations on the subject of African questions. Science, philanthropy, and general policy have had their representatives at these meetings: meetings, the exceptional character of which has been intensified by the presidency of a king. The geographical societies of five foreign nations had sent to Brussels, either their presidents or vice-presidents; that of Italy sent one of its founders. Independently of this element, Germany reckoned a group of its most illustrious travellers; Austria had an eminent statesman, a philanthropist, full of sympathy with every generous sentiment, and a young and courageous traveller; France brought both the theoretical science and the practical experience of African expeditions; England united in ten men, most of whom were of European celebrity, the knowledge of travel and political wisdom, with the most active and the most inexhaustible charity.

The Belgian deputation held a separate situation and had a different part to act. It was concentrated in the person of the King, the chief, the organiser and the initiator of the undertaking. Its special mission was rather outside, than within, the Conference, where courtesy bade it to keep in the background. This does not mean that its presence was to be fruitless in the course of the consultations. In the discussions of the committees, of which no trace has been kept in the *procès verbaux*, the Belgian delegates were able to give full effect to their own views and propositions; but their main action was to be exerted in another direction. In some respects it preceded the calling together of the assembly, and it must survive it, in order to constitute one of the essential pieces of machinery in the execution of its programme, if the glorious task which the Sovereign of Belgium has conceived for his country should be converted into a reality, and if Brussels should truly become—to quote his happy expression—" the head-quarters of this beneficent movement."

The constituent elements of the Conference must not be confounded with the principles of the organisation which has to give movement and life to the work. This organisation comprises three fundamental pieces of machinery: an international commission, an executive committee, and national committees. The composition, duties, and relative positions of these different bodies will be as follows.

The international commission is the parliament of the association. It is composed, in the terms of the resolutions adopted by the Conference, of the presidents of the principal geographical societies represented at Brussels, or accepting its programme, and of two members delegated by each national committee. Although in this latter respect it is only an emanation from the national committees, the commission is above them; it holds the superior direction of the association, and decides all essential questions relating to its constitution or its development. The president has the exercise of extensive powers; he receives into the association the national committees of countries which have not taken part in the deliberations of the Conference; he has the power to fill up the commission itself by adding to its effective and honorary members. The object of this last faculty is to adapt the representation of each country to its proportionate importance in the services rendered to the undertaking. In the exercise of its constituent prerogative, the assembly has deferred the presidency of the international commission to the King of the Belgians for the first period of its existence.

The commission having occasion to meet but at infrequent intervals, it became necessary to establish a permanent medium which should represent it, and take upon itself to carry the resolutions into effect: such is the mission of the executive committee. This body is composed of the president of the international commission, who sits thereat under this same title; of three or four members designated the first time by the Conference, subsequently by the commission; and of a secretary-general named by the president. The latter acquires also, by the fact of his nomination, a seat and a voice in the international commission. The members of the committee are bound to answer at all times the summons of the president: it is the governing power of the association, the heart of its organisation, from which its central and continuous operations proceed. In the terms of the statutes, it will have for its mission " to direct the enterprises and labours tending to achieve the purpose of the association, and to administer the funds supplied by the governments, by the national committees, and by individuals."

The Conference could not dissolve without appointing a directing body. It has named, as members of the executive committee, Sir Bartle Frere, Dr. Nachtigal, and M. de Quatrefages. Sir Bartle Frere is one of the most eminent of English statesmen; he has recently distinguished himself by his mission to the Sultan of Zanzibar, and by the negotiation of a treaty intended to fix upon the broadest bases the abolition of the slave trade. Dr. Nachtigal ranks among the first of African explorers; his great expedition into the Soudan has gained him a prominent place in history. M. de Quatrefages is one of the most learned naturalists of the age, and is at the present moment Vice-President of the Society of Geography of Paris.

The national committees are the third element in the system organised by the Conference; they are the popular basis of the work, the instruments of its mission, the foundation of its resources. The national committees need not be constructed upon an uniform model; each country may decide, according to its own taste, the method of organisation; but in all cases they will have the same mission to fulfil. This mission cannot fail to be admirable and important. It will have within its scope the familiarising in every way the popular mind with all ideas connected with Africa, to make known its physical and ethnographical conditions, its wants and its resources, its splendour and its suffering. It will have to interest in the work and in the heroic enterprises of travellers a number of people who are only apathetic because they are ignorant, and to draw the sympathies of the public to the millions of men who up to the present time have lived excluded from the benefits of civilisation, or have only known it by the evils inflicted upon them by the most unworthy of its representatives. Lastly, its work will be to excite a spirit of sacrifice and devotion; to beg and obtain from all directions a generous and continuous pecuniary support. The African subscription, under the popular form assigned to it by the king, may make the tour of the world, and never shall charity have sown on its surface holier or more fruitful seed.

It would be useless to go further into the details of this system of organisation;* suffice it to say that the general details are well planned and understood. At the very moment when we write these lines the germs

* See the text of the resolutions of the Conference on this subject, in Appendix IV.

of committees are forming in several parts of Europe; they will have to appeal to individual energy, they will have to utilise, in order to attain the common object, all that they shall find ready to their hand, in the way of constituted bodies, whether learned, artistic, or even simply banded societies, among the different nations. Here a consideration presents itself on which we must pause for a moment. The Conference of Brussels, and the international association which takes its origin from it, have had, and still have a private character: is it to be said that the governments of civilised nations are to be absolutely excluded from all interest in these questions? We think not; and without prejudice to any other considerations which may be suggested by political wisdom and foresight, historical precedents bear out this opinion.

In the beginning of the year 1815, the plenipotentiaries of eight powers, assembled in congress at Vienna, had to give a decision, in virtue of the initiative taken by Great Britain and France, on the question of the *universal and definitive abolition* of the slave trade. This movement met with a warm support, the declaration of which, on the 8th of February, contains the following eloquent utterance:—

"It being understood," says this document, "that the traffic known by the name of the Traite des Nègres d'Afrique has been regarded by just and enlightened men of all times as repugnant to the principles of humanity and universal morality . . . That the plenipotentiaries assembled in the congress, could not more effectually do honour to their mission and fulfil their duty than by proclaiming in the names of their sovereigns their desire to put an end to a scourge which has for so long desolated Africa, degraded Europe, and afflicted humanity . . . Consequently, and being duly authorised in this course by the unanimous consent of their respective courts, . . . they declare, in the presence of all Europe, that regarding the *universal abolition* of the slave trade, as a measure peculiarly worthy of their attention, conformable to the spirit of the age, and to the generous principles of their august sovereigns, *they are animated by a sincere desire to effect the most prompt and efficacious execution of this measure, by every means in their power*, and to act, in the employment of these means, with all the zeal and all the perseverance which they owe to so great and noble a cause."

This declaration bears, among others, the signatures of Castlereagh, Wellington, Nesselrode, Humboldt, Metternich, and Talleyrand.

Seven years afterwards, on the 28th of November, 1822, the plenipotentiaries of the five great powers solemnly renewed these engagements at the Congress of Verona. They laid it down that the slave trade, although proscribed, " has continued to this day ; that it has gained in intensity what it may have lost in extent ; that it has even assumed a more odious and deadly character from the nature of the means to which those who exercise it are forced to have recourse ; that thousands of human beings become from year to year its innocent victims. They declare, in consequence, *that they are ready to lend their support to anything that may tend to secure and accelerate the complete and definite abolition of this trade.*"

Half a century has passed since this language was held; and it may be judged by the picture which has been drawn above, whether the powers have gained their end, and whether they may consider themselves as freed from the obligations which they had contracted. The maritime states, especially England, have made energetic and persevering efforts; but there exists in the present day a universal conviction that the most active cruising is useless, and that the trade can only be destroyed on the actual scene of its outrages. Such is, in fact, one of the essential aims pursued by the international association; in opening up Africa to science, Christianity, commerce, and civilisation, it adopts the true and only system which, by consent of all travellers, can result in the *complete and definitive abolition* of the slave trade. Consequently it is the programme of all Europe which it carries out, and what more just, therefore, than to see all governments lend it their sympathetic support? It is not our place here to determine the form which their assistance may take; it may, according to place and circumstance, assume divers forms; but, supposing it only to be sincere, energetic and sustained, is it too much to hope favourably of a work which responds, in every object which it purposes, to the highest aspirations of the age? If these hopes come to be realised, the association will acquire at the outset a broad and solid foundation. Perhaps, if powerfully assisted at the same time by private benevolence, it may begin from several points at once the execution of its purpose. Under these conditions, the final success of the enterprise does not admit of a single doubt, and the operations in Africa will receive an impulse, the consequences of which cannot fail to be felt in the most divergent directions.

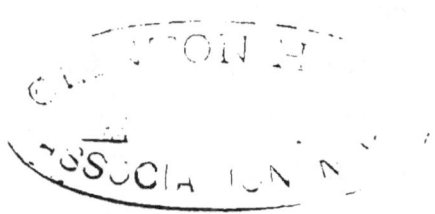

CHAPTER VII.

CONCLUSION.

If what has been just read has been successful in conveying at least some vague notion of the object of this undertaking, it will have justified the high expectations to which expression was given at the close of the debates of the Conference. To achieve the scientific exploration of Africa, to carry into it light and civilisation, to spread therein the ideas and the products of Christian nations, above all, to prosecute with invincible energy the suppression of the slave trade; this, it has been thought, was to formulate a programme in harmony with the wishes of all nations. Kindly in its purpose, the enterprise has seemed justified in counting on their assistance, all the more, that its execution made no appeal to force, and looked only to moral influence, persuasion, devotedness, and individual generosity. Can this confidence have been overweening? Can an assembly composed of so many specially selected men, at which sat so many competent judges, so many men who spoke from their own experience, have been the dupe of a beautiful but vain Utopia? Who would venture to say so? Who would willingly think so? No; the conclusion that the Conference has arrived at has been founded on a firm reality. Its work has not been built upon the sand; it contains the germ of a grand future, because it is inspired with thoughts and is addressed to feelings which form the living principle of modern communities, and the diffusion of which is as necessary as it is justifiable. To grasp these moral forces, to group them in a powerful organisation, to indicate to them an object as worthy of tempting, as it is capable of recompensing, their efforts; in this we have a task, vast no doubt, but not unrealisable, the accomplishment of which it has been thought might be trusted to the combination of all civilised nations meeting together on this common ground.

It is true that, even seconded as it must be, by the prevailing currents of thought which influence mankind at the present time, this task will still be long and laborious: yet, at the same time, it possesses special attractions calculated to support zeal and encourage self-devotion. In fact, what undertaking fulfils to a higher degree all the conditions requisite for popular success? Have not the labours of travellers going forth for the discovery of distant lands, braving all dangers and all sufferings, in order to open up new fields of civilisation, always possessed the gift of exciting the curiosity and the admiration of the masses? What story exceeds in interest the narrative of their heroic adventures? With what transports of enthusiasm is not their happy return welcomed in every country after some daring and successful campaign? What feeling more natural than that of wishing to associate ourselves with their efforts, and to help on their achievements. These feelings belong to all times and to all places; they are not peculiar to scientific men who follow the steps of explorers with an attentive and anxious eye: they are entertained by all enlightened minds which are open to generous ideas and sympathise with manly undertakings.

Now what land is more suited by its marvels to realise the flights of imagination than this immense Africa,—so near to us in actual distance, seen only by glimpses throughout the succession of ages, where nature has been pleased to accumulate all her magnificence, to display all the splendour of her contrasts, where, by a melancholy contradiction, history has for ages past written the most sinister, the most shameful pages of her annals? For—and this is a characteristic trait of this noble work—it interests the heart at least as much as it fascinates the mind. Every step forward in the way of science will be here a step forward in the way of justice; every obstacle that is removed will speak of chains being broken, and no where will light prove to such a degree the parent of liberty—liberty in its humblest, but also its holiest acceptation—liberty which means the in-born right of men to their own existence, and to the possession of their own persons, their own labour, and their own children.

From whatever side, then, we view it, the enterprise which occupies our attention is alive with noble impulses and suggests grand thoughts. What if, anticipating the future, we were to contemplate in advance the total result; what a spectacle would be presented to the eyes of the man of science, as well as of the statesman! If directed with unity of view and harmony in operation, and if supplied with plentiful resources, the geographical exploration of the hitherto unknown regions of Africa will be completed before the close of this century. The present generation will not disappear without having seen the entire map of the continent, if not perfect in its minute details, at least correct in its general features.

The conquests of civilisation will have followed close on those of science. The stations after having been points of support and refuge for the explorers, will become focuses of light, and centres of so many groups of races, gradually rising, under their auspices, to social conditions of a higher order. Religious missions, now confined to the coasts, will be able to penetrate into the interior, and sow the seed of the gospel in a soil which, more than any other, promises abundant harvests. Under the combined influence of these civilising agencies, the fountain-head of the slave trade will be dried up; the progressive diminution of its ravages, by increasing the security of the natives, will give scope to the growing communities of Central Africa to develope themselves without hindrance. Thanks to the establishment of extensive and distant commercial relations, their material prosperity would soon acquire a broad and stable basis. Before fifty years from this time it would not be impossible that Africa should become one of the great markets producing some of the primary materials of European industry, and she would then necessarily absorb in a proportionate degree considerable quantities of manufactured goods. Much physical and moral force, now unemployed in the countries of Europe, will then be able to find useful and profitable modes of application on this new soil. The combined efforts of so many men of different nationality will create among the states of the Old World an additional bond of solidarity, and, in its enlarged domain, mankind will henceforth see all the races of the globe co-operating towards the fulfilment of its destinies. Such is in substance the picture which history has already partially drawn since the discovery of America and of Oceania; it may be renewed before our eyes in Africa, but under conditions more complete, and, at the same time, more worthy of the civilisation of our age, without being disfigured either by the spirit of conquest, which has been the source of so many bloody rivalries, nor by the criminal excesses of which the native populations were in the sixteenth century the unhappy victims, nor by the mistakes in economy, which have so often smitten with sterility the richest gifts of Providence.

These views are no longer those of a small number of men; they spread from place to place, and rapidly gain the masses. This accounts for the sympathetic echo which has so promptly responded from all countries to the initiative taken at Brussels. Already England, Germany, France, and Russia have set to work. Centres of action, in connection with the general direction, are being formed in the principal nations of Europe. In the constitution of national committees, now definitely settled, the Conference sees an essential element of its programme converted into a reality, and an immediate and indispensable means of bringing into play the organs which itself has created.

Belgium—significant symptoms bear testimony to the fact—will hold it a point of honour not to allow herself to be outrun in this race; she will not remain behind other nations, either in the extent of the sacrifices which she will impose upon herself in order to give a broad material foundation to the undertaking, or in the unflagging zeal which she will bring to bear for its support and extension. No element is wanting for the well fulfilling of her task; she possesses riches, she has science at her disposal, and men eager for work outside their own country, on which to exert their superabundant energies and talents. Being capable of action, Belgium has every interest in acting; while she finds in Africa a vast field of expansion, which invites her activity in every direction, she may assume in Europe an attitude which will not be without a certain moral dignity. Higher considerations still will not find her indifferent: she has in this position duties to fulfil towards herself. She will remember the proud traditions of her past, when her banner waved both on land and sea in the advanced guard of civilising enterprises. She will not allow the glorious mission which has been assigned to her by the initiation of her sovereign to dwindle in her hands. Above all, she will not forget that the nations of Europe, in making her capital the centre of their united action, give her a proof of esteem and confidence, which it is the duty of a generous nation to be heartily grateful for.

APPENDIX.

I.

MEMBERS OF THE BRUSSELS GEOGRAPHICAL CONFERENCE.

(12, 13, AND 14 SEPTEMBER, 1876).

APPENDIX.

I.

MEMBERS OF THE BRUSSELS GEOGRAPHICAL CONFERENCE.

(12, 13, AND 14 SEPTEMBER, 1876).

THE KING OF THE BELGIANS.

MEMBERS:

FOR GERMANY—
  Baron VON RICHTHOFEN, President of the Geographical Society of Berlin.
  Dr. G. NACHTIGAL.
  Dr. G. ROHLFS, Councillor of the Court of Prussia.
  Dr. G. SCHWEINFURTH.

FOR AUSTRIA-HUNGARY—
  Baron HOFMANN, Privy Councillor, Minister of Finance of the Empire.
  Count ED. ZICHY, Privy Councillor.
  Dr. F. VON HOCHSTETTER, Court Councillor, Professor at the Upper Institute of Arts and Manufactures, President of the Geographical Society of Vienna.
  First Lieutenant A. LUX.

FOR BELGIUM—

Baron A. LAMBERMONT, Minister Plenipotentiary, Secretary-General of the Department of Foreign Affairs.

M. E. BANNING, Director in the Department of Foreign Affairs.

M. EMILE DE BORCHGRAVE, Councillor of Legation.

M. A. COUVREUR, Member of the Chamber of Representatives.

Count GOBLET D'ALVIELLA, Member of the Provincial Council of Brabant.

M. E. JAMES, Professor in the University of Brussels.

M. E. DE LAVELEYE, Professor in the University of Liege.

M. J. QUAIRIER, Director at the Societé Générale.

M. CH. SAINCTELETTE, Member of the Chamber of Representatives.

M. T. SMOLDERS, Member of the Chamber of Representatives, Professor in the University of Louvain.

M. VAN BIERVLIET.

M. L. VAN DEN BOSSCHE, Councillor of Legation.

M. J. VAN VOLXEM.

FOR FRANCE—

Vice-Admiral Baron DE LA RONCIÈRE-LE-NOURY, Senator, President of the Geographical Society of Paris.

M. MAUNOIR, Secretary-General of the Geographical Society of Paris.

M. H. DUVEYRIER, Assistant-Secretary of the Geographical Society of Paris.

The Marquis DE COMPIÈGNE.

FOR GREAT BRITAIN—

Sir BARTLE FRERE, Vice-President of the Council of India.

Sir RUTHERFORD ALCOCK, Minister Plenipotentiary, President of the Royal Geographical Society of London.

FOR GREAT BRITAIN—*continued.*

Major-General Sir HENRY RAWLINSON, Member of the Council of India.
Rear-Admiral Sir LEOPOLD HEATH.
Lt.-Colonel J. A. GRANT.
Commander VERNEY LOVETT CAMERON.
Mr. W. MACKINNON.
Sir T. FOWELL BUXTON.
Sir J. KENNAWAY.
Sir HARRY VERNEY.

FOR ITALY—

The Commendatore C. NEGRI, Minister Plenipotentiary.

FOR RUSSIA—

M. P. DE SEMENOW, President of the Statistical Council, Vice-President of the Geographical Society of St. Petersburg.

The Bureau consisted of the following:—

PRESIDENT:

THE KING OF THE BELGIANS.

VICE-PRESIDENTS:

The Baron VON RICHTHOFEN, President of the Geographical Society of Berlin.
Dr. F. VON HOCHSTETTER, President of the Geographical Society of Vienna.

VICE-PRESIDENTS—*continued.*

Vice-Admiral Baron DE LA RONCIÈRE-LE-NOURY, President of the Geographical Society of Paris.

Sir RUTHERFORD ALCOCK, President of the Geographical Society of London.

SECRETARIES:

M. E. BANNING.   M. E. JAMES.

II.

SPEECH DELIVERED BY THE KING AT THE OPENING OF THE CONFERENCE.

"GENTLEMEN,—Allow me to thank you warmly for the obliging readiness with which you have been so good as to respond to my invitation. Besides the satisfaction I shall have in listening to the discussion of the problems in the solution of which we are interested, I experience the keenest pleasure in meeting with the distinguished men whose labours and courageous exertions in behalf of civilisation I have for several years observed.

"The subject which brings us together to-day is one of those which deserve to take a leading place in engaging the attention of the friends of humanity. To open up to civilisation the only part of our globe which it has not yet penetrated, to pierce the darkness in which entire populations are enveloped, is, I venture to say, a crusade worthy of this age of progress, and I am happy to perceive how much the public feeling is in favour of its accomplishment; the tide is with us.

"Gentlemen, amongst those who have studied Africa the most, a great number have been led to think that it would be advantageous for the common object, that they should aim at bringing about the means of meeting and conferring together, with the view of regulating proceedings, combining efforts, turning to account all resources, and avoiding the waste caused by duplicate labour.

"It has seemed to me that Belgium, a central and neutral state, would be a well-selected country for such a meeting, and this has emboldened me to invite you all here to my palace, to the little Conference which I have the great satisfaction of opening to-day. Need I say that, in bringing you to Brussels, I have not been influenced by selfish views. No, gentlemen, if Belgium is small, she is happy and contented with her lot. I have no other ambition than to serve her well. But I will not go so far as to assert that I should be insensible to the honour which would result to my country from the fact that an important progress in a question which will make its mark in our era, should be dated from Brussels. I should be happy that Brussels became, in some sort, the head-quarters of this civilising movement.

"I have allowed myself then to entertain the thought that it might fall within your convenience to come and discuss, and, with the authority which belongs to you, unitedly to decide upon the roads to follow and the means to employ for definitively planting the standard of civilisation on the soil of Central Africa; to agree upon what ought to be done in order to interest the public in your noble enterprise, and to induce it to aid with its subscriptions. For, gentlemen, in works of this kind, it is the concurrence of the great number which brings success, it is the sympathy of the masses which it is necessary to invite and to succeed in obtaining.

"What resources, in fact, should we not have at our disposal, if all those to whom a franc is nothing, or very little, consented to throw it into the treasury devoted to the suppression of the slave trade in the interior of Africa?

"Great progress has been already made, and the unknown country has been assailed on many sides; and if those here present, who have enriched science with discoveries of so great importance, would retrace for us the principal points of them, their recital would be a powerful encouragement for all.

"Among the questions which remain still to be examined, the following have been specified:

"First. The exact laying down of bases of operation to be acquired, among others, on the coast of Zanzibar, and near the mouth of the Congo, either by stipulation with the chiefs, or by purchase, or by arrangements with private individuals.

"Secondly. The laying down of the routes to be successively opened towards the interior, and of the stations for purposes of relief, of science, and of pacification, which have to be organised, as a means of abolishing slavery, of establishing harmony among the chiefs, and of providing for them just and disinterested arbitrators, etc.

"Thirdly. The creation, so soon as the work shall have been well defined, of an international and central committee and of national committees, to carry out its execution, by each, in its own special direction, making the object desired known in their respective countries, and also by making an appeal to that feeling of charity to which no good cause has ever yet addressed itself in vain.

"Such, gentlemen, are some of the different points which seem to deserve your consideration; if there be others they will evolve themselves in the course of your discussions, and you will not fail to throw light upon them.

"My desire is, to help on, in the manner that you may point out to me, the great cause for which you have already done so much. With this object, I place myself at your disposal, and bid you a hearty welcome."

III.

DECISION OF THE CONFERENCE ON THE SUBJECT OF STATIONS.

In order to attain the objects of the International Conference of Brussels, that is to say, to explore scientifically the unknown parts of Africa, to facilitate the opening of roads by which civilisation may be introduced into the interior of the African Continent, and to find means of suppressing the negro slave trade in Africa, it is necessary:

First. To organise on one common international plan the exploration of the unknown parts of Africa, on the understanding that the region to be explored is to have for its boundaries, eastward and westward, the two seas; southward, the basin of the Zambesi; and northward the frontiers of the new Egyptian territory and independent Soudan. The means best adapted for this exploration will be the employment of a sufficient number of separate travellers starting from different bases of operation.

Secondly. To establish as the bases of these operations a certain number of scientific and relief stations, both on the coasts of Africa, and in the interior of the continent.

Of these stations some will be established, in very limited numbers, on the eastern and western coasts of Africa, at points where European civilisation is already represented, as for example, at Bagamoyo and at Loanda. The stations should have the character of depôts provided with the means of supplying travellers with the necessaries of existence and for exploration. They might be established at small expense, for they would be intrusted to the charge of the Europeans residing at these points.

The other stations could be established at points in the interior best adapted to serve as direct bases for explorations. The establishment of these latter stations could be commenced at the points which at the present time recommend themselves as the most favourable for the proposed purpose. For example, Ujiji, Nyangwe, the residence of the king, or some point lying within the domains of Muata-Yamvo, might be specified. The explorers would be able afterwards to point out other positions where it would be convenient to set up similar stations.

Leaving to the future the care of establishing safe communications between the stations, the Conference above all expresses the desire that a line of communication as unbroken as possible should be established from one ocean to the other, following approximately the route of Commander Cameron. The Conference also expresses the hope that lines of operation will be subsequently established in the direction of from north to south.

The Conference requests the good-will and co-operation of all travellers, who henceforward shall undertake scientific explorations in Africa, whether they travel under the auspices of the international commission instituted by its agency, or not.

IV.

RESOLUTIONS OF THE CONFERENCE CONCERNING THE SYSTEM OF ORGANISATION.

1. There shall be established an international commission of exploration and civilisation of Central Africa, and national committees which shall keep themselves in communication with the commission with the view of centralising, as far as possible, the efforts made by their fellow-countrymen, and to facilitate, by their co-operation, the execution of the resolutions of the commission.

2. The national committees constitute themselves in such manner as may seem to them preferable.

3. The commission shall be composed of the presidents of the principal geographical societies which are represented at the Conference of Brussels, or who may subsequently give in their adherence to its programme, and of two members chosen by each national committee.

4. The president shall have the power to admit into the association countries which were not represented at the Conference.

5. The president shall have the power of filling up the international commission by adding to it effective members and honorary members.

6. The central committee, after having drawn up its regulations, shall make it its duty to direct by means of an executive committee the enterprises and operations aiming at the fulfilment of the object of the association and to administer the funds supplied by government, by the national committees and by individuals.

7. The executive committee shall be appointed under the president, and shall consist of three or four members nominated beforehand by the present Conference and subsequently by the international committee.

8. The members of the committee shall hold themselves in readiness to answer to the summons of the president.

9. The president appoints a secretary-general, who by the very fact of his nomination will become a member of the international commission and of the executive committee; the president also appoints a treasurer.

V.

THE CONGRESS OF VIENNA.

Declaration of the Plenipotentiaries of the Powers who Signed the Treaty of Paris of the 30th of May, 1814, relative to the Abolition of the Traite des Nègres d'Afrique, or the Slave Trade.

THE Plenipotentiaries of the Powers who signed the Treaty of Paris of the 30th of May, 1814, assembled in conference, having taken into consideration that the traffic known by the name of Traite des Nègres d'Afrique has been regarded by just and enlightened men of all times as repugnant to the principles of humanity and universal morality;

That the particular circumstances to which this traffic owed its origin, and the difficulty of putting a sudden check upon its progress have, up to a certain point, succeeded in hiding from view the hatefulness of its continuation; but that at length the public voice has been raised in every civilised country to demand its suppression as soon as possible;

That, since the character and details of this traffic have become better known, and the evils of every kind which accompany it have been completely exposed, several European Governments have, in fact, resolved to put a stop to it, and that one after the other all the powers possessing colonies in the different parts of the world, have, either by legislative acts, or by treaties and other formal engagements, recognised the obligation and the necessity of abolishing it;

That, by a separate article of the last Treaty of Paris, Great Britain and France pledged themselves to unite their efforts at the congress of Vienna to induce all the powers of Christendom to declare for the universal and definitive abolition of the slave trade;

That the plenipotentiaries assembled in this congress could not more effectually do honour to their mission, fulfil their duty, and set forth the principles which influence their august sovereigns than by striving to realise this engagement and by proclaiming in the name of their sovereigns, the desire to put an end to a scourge which for so long a time has desolated Africa, degraded Europe and afflicted humanity;

The said plenipotentiaries are agreed to open their deliberations on the means of accomplishing so salutary an object by a formal declaration of the principles which have influenced them in this work.

Consequently, and being duly authorised in this course by the unanimous consent of their respective courts, they declare in the presence of all Europe that, regarding the universal abolition of the slave trade as a measure peculiarly worthy of their attention, and conformable to the spirit of the age and to the generous principles of their august sovereigns, they are animated by a sincere desire to effect the most prompt and efficacious execution of this measure by every means in their power, and to act, in the employment of these means, with all the zeal and all the perseverance which they owe to so great and so noble a cause.

Being, however, too well acquainted with the sentiments of their sovereigns not to foresee that however honourable their objects, they must not pursue it without just consideration for the interests, habits, and even prejudices of their subjects, the said plenipotentiaries at the same time recognise it as a principle that this general declaration is not to prejudge the period which each power in particular may regard as most convenient for the definitive abolition of the traffic in negroes: Consequently, the determination of the time when this traffic must universally cease, will be a subject of negotiation between the powers; it being well understood that no means will be neglected which are adapted to ensure and to accelerate the movement, and that the mutual engagement contracted by the present declaration between the sovereigns who have taken part in it, will not be considered as fulfilled until the moment when complete success shall have crowned their united efforts.

In bringing this declaration to the knowledge of Europe and of all the civilised nations of the world the said plenipotentiaries hope to induce all other governments, and especially those which, in the abolition of the slave trade, have already given proof of the same feelings, to support them with their concurrence in a cause the final triumph of which will be one of the noblest monuments of the age which has undertaken it and which will have brought it to so glorious a completion.

Vienna, the 8th of February, 1815.

(Signed)	CASTLEREAGH.	PALMELLA.
	STEWART.	SALDANHA.
	WELLINGTON.	LOBO.
	NESSELRODE.	HUMBOLDT.
	C. LOEWENHIELM.	METTERNICH.
	GOMEZ LABRADOR.	TALLEYRAND.

VI.

CONGRESS OF VERONA.

Declaration of the 28th of November, 1822, on the Abolition of the Traite des Nègres d'Afrique.

THE Plenipotentiaries of Austria, of France, of Great Britain, of Prussia and of Russia, assembled in Congress at Verona;

Taking into consideration, that their august sovereigns have taken part in the declaration of the 8th of February, 1815, by which the powers assembled in congress at Vienna, proclaimed in the face of Europe their unalterable resolution to put an end to the traffic known under the name of Traite des Nègres d'Afrique;

Taking moreover into consideration that, notwithstanding this declaration, and in spite of the legislative measures by which it has been followed in many countries, and of the different treaties concluded since the said period between the maritime powers, this traffic, formally proscribed, has continued to this very day; that it has gained in intensity what it may have lost in extent, that it has even assumed a more hateful and more sinister character from the nature of the means to which those who carry it on have been compelled to have recourse; that the causes of so revolting an abuse, are principally to be found in the fraudulent practices by which the undertakers of these condemnable speculations evade the laws of their country, baffle the surveillance of the vessels employed to arrest the progress of their iniquities, and hide from view the criminal operations of which thousands of human beings become the yearly victims;

That the powers of Europe are called upon by their previous engagements, as well as by a sacred duty, to seek the most effective means of preventing a traffic which has already been pronounced unlawful and culpable by the laws of almost every civilised country, and severely to punish those who prosecute it in open contravention of those laws;

Have recognised the necessity of devoting the most serious attention to an object of such great importance to the well-being and honour of humanity, and, consequently, they declare in the name of their august sovereigns, that they unalterably persist in the same principles and sentiments which these sovereigns manifested by the declaration of the 8th of February,

1815;—That they have not ceased, and will never cease to regard the trade in negroes as a scourge which has too long desolated Africa, degraded Europe, and afflicted humanity, and that they are ready to concur in everything which may insure and accelerate the complete and definitive abolition of this traffic.

That in order to give effect to this renewed declaration, their respective cabinets will devote themselves with earnestness to the seeking out of every measure compatible with their rights and the interests of their subjects to bring about a result, which shall prove in the eyes of the world the sincerity of their desires and of their efforts in favour of a cause deserving of their united solicitude.

Verona, the 28th of November, 1822.

(Signed) METTERNICH.   WELLINGTON.
LEBZELTERN.   HATZFELDT.
CHÂTEAUBRIAND.   NESSELRODE.
CARAMAN.   LIEVEN.
FERRONAIS.   TATISCHEFF.

VII.

ADDRESS DELIVERED BY THE KING AT THE MEETING FOR INSTALLING THE BELGIAN COMMITTEE, HELD ON THE 6TH OF NOVEMBER, 1876, IN THE PALACE AT BRUSSELS.

"GENTLEMEN,—The slavery which is still continued over a considerable portion of the African Continent is a plague-spot which all friends of civilisation must desire to see obliterated.

"The horrors of this state of things, the thousands of victims which the slave trade causes to be massacred every year, the still greater number of perfectly innocent beings who are brutally dragged into captivity and condemned wholesale to hard labour for life, have keenly touched the feelings of all those who have in any degree studied with attention this deplorable reality, and they have conceived the idea of combining, of co-operating and, in one word, of founding an international association to put a stop to an odious traffic, which is a disgrace to the age in which we live, and to tear away the veil of darkness which still hangs over Central Africa. The discoveries for which we are indebted to brave explorers, enable us now to say that it is one of the fairest and richest countries that God has created.

"The Brussels Conference has named a committee of three members: Sir Bartle Frere, Dr. Nachtigal and M. de Quatrefages, of the Institute of France, to put in execution, in conjunction with the presidents and secretary-general, the declarations and resolutions which it has formulated as follows * :—

"The Conference has desired, with the view of bringing it into closer relations with the public, whose sympathy will be our strength, to found national committees in each country. These committees, after having each delegated two members to take part in the international committee, will give publicity in their respective countries to the programme adopted.

"The undertaking has already received in France and in Belgium important subscriptions, to the givers of which we owe a debt of gratitude. These acts of charity, so honourable to the doers, are a stimulus to our zeal in the task which we have undertaken. Our first endeavour must be to reach the heart of the masses, and, as the numbers increase, to bring together our

* For the text of these documents, see Appendix III. and IV.

adherents into a fraternal union, which, while it will weigh but lightly on each side, will be powerful and fruitful by means of the combination of individual efforts and their results.

"The international association does not pretend to take upon itself all the good that can, and ought to be done in Africa. It must, especially at first, deny to itself a very extended programme: but supported by public sympathy, we are convinced that if we succeed in opening roads, and in establishing stations on the tracks followed by the slave merchants, this odious traffic will be put a stop to, and the stations, while serving as points of relief for travellers, will powerfully help in the evangelisation of the negroes, and in the introduction amongst them of commerce and modern industrial occupations. We unhesitatingly assert that all who wish the enfranchisement of the black race are interested in our success.

"The Belgian committee, emanating from the international committee and representing it in Belgium, will make every effort to gain the greatest possible number of adherents to the undertaking. It will assist my fellow-countrymen in once more proving, that Belgium is not only a land of hospitality, but that she is also a generous nation in which the cause of humanity finds as many defenders as she can count citizens.

"I fulfil a very agreeable duty, when I thank this assembly, and warmly congratulate it on having undertaken a task, the completion of which will contribute to our country's glory one fair page more in the annals of charity and of progress."

APPENDIX.

VIII.

INTERNATIONAL ASSOCIATION FOR THE SUPPRESSION OF THE SLAVE TRADE AND OPENING UP CENTRAL AFRICA.

STATUTES OF THE BELGIAN NATIONAL COMMITTEE.

Article 1. A national committee has been established at Brussels charged with the carrying into execution, as far as itself is concerned and within the limits of Belgium, the programme of the International Conference for the suppression of the slave trade, and the exploration of Africa.

Article 2. This programme, according to the views of the Belgian Committee, may be summed up in the two following points:—

(*a*). To make known in Belgium, both by word of mouth and by the press, all the information of every kind which bears upon the object which the international association has in view.

(*b*). To organise a national subscription, and to centralise the resources of every kind which may be placed at their disposal, for the execution of the international programme.

Article 3. The Belgian committee consists of persons who have accepted the invitation to be present at the meeting of to-day.

Article 4. The committee nominates the members of its own bureau, which consists of a president, two vice-presidents, and two delegates representing the committee at the international commission, the secretary-general, and the treasurer of the executive committee, and an assistant secretary.

The bureau, if it thinks fit, can add to itself two supplementary members.

In the absence of the president, each of the vice-presidents is called upon alternately to preside.

Article 5. The bureau will have the right to add to the present members of the committee, such persons as shall have rendered signal services to the undertaking, and those whose co-operation would be particularly serviceable to it.

The bureau represents the Belgian committee in the intervals of its meetings; it is its executive organ, and may be summoned by the president whenever he may deem it convenient.

Besides these occasions, the bureau meets regularly once a month, at least, at the office of the association. The strictly administrative work is assigned to the secretary-general and the treasurer, who refer to the president whenever occasion requires it.

Article 6. The duration of the functions of the president, the vice-presidents, and the two members delegate, is three years. These officers are re-eligible.

The committee nominates its own secretary, and its own treasurer. Their habitual residence must be in Brussels.

The functions of president, vice-president, member delegate, secretary, and treasurer are gratuitous.

The secretary receives the communications which are addressed to the committee: the treasurer the funds placed at the disposal of the committee.

Of these funds, such part as the bureau shall judge strictly necessary for the expenses of the national committee shall remain appropriated to that special purpose: the remainder shall be handed over to the treasurer of the international undertaking who will negotiate its investment, and hold the revenue at the disposal of the executive international committee.

Article 7. The local committees which may hereafter be established in the country, shall, as far as possible, be centralised in the province, except in Brabant, where the national committee sits. They will hold themselves in constant communication with the national committee, from which they take their instructions, and to which they make a monthly remittance of the funds collected through their exertions.

Article 8. The national committee, through the medium of its bureau, corresponds, for the purposes of the undertaking, with public authorities, private associations, and individuals.

Article 9. The national committee nominates two members of the international commission: the appointment of these delegates lasts for three years; these officers are re-eligible.

Article 10. In the execution of its duties, the national committee informs itself of the views, and conforms itself to the instructions of the international commission and of the executive committee with which it will hold itself in regular communication.

Article 11. The national committee meets at Brussels at the summons of its president.

Article 12. The members of the national committee contribute to the undertaking by an annual contribution according to their means, or by some work conducive to the general object.

Article 13. Every year, on the 1st of March, the committee meets in formal public assembly for the purpose of receiving the report of the secretary-general and of the treasurer, and of taking into consideration every thing which may be of advantage to the undertaking, as well as of giving expansion to opinions relative to the duties undertaken, and to the amount of progress realised by the international association.

Article 14. A copy of all the publications which may be issued, either by the international commission, or by the executive committee, or by the national committee, shall be sent, through the latter, to each of its members. Copies shall also be placed at the disposal of the provincial committees.

Article 15. The national committee shall have power to confer honorary diplomas and medals on such persons both within or outside of the association as shall have rendered exceptional services to the undertaking. The conferment of these diplomas, and medals, shall take place every year at the formal public meeting provided by Article 13.

Article 16. The national committee shall have power to introduce into the regulatory arrangements of the present statutes such modifications as experience may show to be desirable, but which must be in harmony with the declarations and resolutions of the Brussels Conference.

Read and adopted at the meeting of the 6th November, 1876.

IX.

MEMBERS OF THE BELGIUM INTERNATIONAL COMMITTEE.

PRESIDENT:

H. R. H. THE COUNT OF FLANDERS.

VICE-PRESIDENTS:

Baron D'ANETHAN, Minister of State, and Senator.
M. H. DOLEZ, Minister of State, and Senator.

Delegates to the International Commission:

Baron LAMBERMONT, Minister Plenipotentiary, Secretary-General of the Department for Foreign Affairs.

General LIAGRE, Commandant of the Military School, Perpetual Secretary of the Academy.

SECRETARY:

Baron GREINDL, Minister Plenipotentiary.

TREASURER:

M. GALEZOT, Sub-Director of the Finance Department.

MEMBERS:

Major ADAN, Second Commandant of the Military College.

M. ANSPACH, Representative, Mayor of Brussels.

Count Charles D'ASPREMONT-LYNDEN, Member of the Provincial Council of the province of Namur.

M. BANNING, Director of the Department for Foreign Affairs.

M. BISCHOFFSHEIM, Senator.

M. BRACONIER, Senator.

M. Cannart d'Hamale, Senator.
Baron Constantine de Caters, Ship-owner.
M. Couvreur, Representative.
M. Crombez, Representative, Mayor of Tournai.
M. de Becker, Advocate of the Court of Cassation.
M. Em. de Laveleye, Professor at the University of Liége.
M. Delloye-Mathieu, Mayor of Huy.
M. de Rongé, Councillor of the Court of Cassation.
M. Gheeland, Member of the Provincial Council of the province of Antwerp.
Count Goblet d'Alviella, Member of the Provincial Council of the province of Brabant.
M. Houzeau, Director of the Observatory, Member of the Academy.
M. James, Professor at the University of Brussels.
Colonel Baron F. Jolly, Commandant of the Military College.
Baron Kervyn de Volkaersbeke, Representative.
M. Lefebvre, Representative.
M. Leclercq, Advocate at the Court of Cassation.
M. Lemmé, formerly Member of the Chamber of Commerce of Antwerp.
M. Linden, Naturalist, Consul-General.
Baron de Montblanc, Representative.
M. Orban de Xivry, Senator.
Count d'Oultremont de Warfusée, Member of the Provincial Council of the province of Liége.
M. Parmentier, Manufacturer.
M. Picard, President of the Provincial Council of the province of Brabant.
M. Quairier, Director of the Société Générale.
M. Sabatier, Representative.
M. Sadoine, Director of John Cockerill's works at Seraing.

M. SAINCTELETTE, Representative.
M. SAINT-PAUL-DE-SINÇAY, Managing Director of the Société de la Vieille Montagne.
M. SCHOLLAERT, Representative.
M. SMOLDERS, Representative.
M. SOLVYNS, Senator.
M. TRASENSTER, Professor at the University of Liége.
M. VAN BENEDEN, Professor at the University of Louvain, Member of the Academy.
M. VAN BIERVLIET, Advocate.
M. VAN DEN BOSSCHE, Councillor of Legation, Chief of the Cabinet of the Department of Foreign Affairs.
M. VAN DER STICHELEN, formerly Minister for Foreign Affairs and Public Works.
M. VAN HOEGAERDEN, Director at the National Bank.
M. VAN SCHELLE, Advocate.
M. VAN VOLXEM, Proprietor.
M. WAROCQUÉ, Representative.
Baron GUSTAVE DE WOELMONT, Senator.
Baron GUSTAVE VAN DE WOESTYNE, Senator.

THE END.

EPILOGUE.*

Since the preceding pages were written and published, several new and important documents concerning Africa have made their appearance. Among them are two which have been received everywhere with extreme interest, and would seem to be of a character to exercise peculiar influence on public opinion in England. The first of these documents is a lecture delivered before the Chamber of Commerce at Cape Town by Lieutenant Young, R.N., on his return from the Livingstonia Expedition on the shores of the Lake Nyassa; the second is no other than Commander Cameron's Narrative of his Voyage across Africa.

The Report of Lieutenant Young circumstantially and conclusively proves what great results it is possible to obtain, both for the civilisation of the negroes and the suppression of the slave trade, as the sole result of moral influence and of enlightened and kindly patronage without any resort to force. The facts

* Written in March, 1877.

which it specifies confirm, with singular precision, several of the leading points in our book. In another direction Commander Cameron presents us, as the conclusion to his work, with an assemblage of remarks and of views, which, coming from so clear-sighted and experienced a traveller, constitute important testimony in favour of the generous and practical character of the undertaking set on foot by the Brussels Conference.

In view of these facts, it will not be amiss to give here some quotations from each of these publications, in which are strongly exhibited, as over-riding all personal or national prejudices, those noble and truly Christian feelings which, on these questions, have at all times actuated the English nation.

"The expedition," says Lieutenant Young, "had been quite successful in everything they took in hand. Everything, in fact, had exceeded his expectations. The expedition was in possession of Lake Nyassa, and had established a good name there. They had made friends with every one, and enemies with no one. . . . As for the mission, it was firmly and satisfactorily established on the lake, and had already made itself felt. He had orders not to interfere with the slave trade, but indirectly a great check had been put upon it. Formerly not fewer than 10,000 slaves passed the southern end of the lake per annum, but last year only thirty-eight were known to have succeeded in getting to the coast by that route. Thus far, therefore, the Livingstonia Expedition had been the means of saving the lands from slavery, and not only so, but as soon as it was known that the English had come there, the people flocked back, and built villages on the side of the lake. If they asked them, 'Why are you doing so?' the reply was, 'The English are come, and we are quite satisfied.'

"As for the country, it was the finest he had ever seen. The Nyassa was called a lake, but it was in fact a vast inland sea. The native canoes never thought of crossing the lake, but they went along its shores. It was not so densely populated now as when Livingstone first discovered it; but nothing would be easier than to develop its resources and to open up trade. He did not altogether believe in missionaries going in for trade, but, nevertheless, it must be introduced, and the banks of the upper shore would supply all the world with cotton and sugar. The natives were very willing, and with a little encouragement could easily be made to produce very largely. He found they obeyed him with alacrity, and readily acknowledged him as head, because they knew he was English. . . . When the last steamer went up, he said that he required 1000 natives on a certain day, and they were there. They never asked what they were going to receive, and they carried heavy loads without injuring or losing anything. They found themselves in provisions, and when they went home he paid them each six yards of calico, with which they were quite satisfied. When he came down to meet Dr. Stewart, he returned with 500 carriers, and on this occasion he paid them only four yards of calico each. The English name was good, and the natives were ready to do whatever they were told. The pure African, not spoilt by the European, they could mould into any shape they liked.

Lake Nyassa was a deep basin; it was deep all over. On the north-east shores a range of very high mountains ran parallel with the lake for upwards of 100 miles. Their height was from 10,000 feet to 12,000 feet, and they came down very steeply to the margin. Table Mountain would look quite insignificant beside them. During his voyage of circumnavigation, a heavy gale of wind was experienced, which compelled them to lay to for two days. The attempt to sound one part of the lake a quarter of a mile from shore with 140 fathoms of line failed to get bottom at that depth. The mission had nothing to complain of. The lake teemed with fish, and plenty of fowls, goats, and sheep were to be had, and there would soon be oxen. For some 800 miles the coast was a beautiful country. An Englishman could live there as well as in Cape Town.

"He might say that the Zambezi and its tributaries were a mine of wealth, and all that was wanted was men of energy and enterprise to develop it. As to the mission, there had not been a hitch of any kind. Everything had succeeded better than he expected, and he looked for better things yet. If a more suitable man could not be got, he was quite ready and willing to go and do what was necessary himself. In reply to questions put to him, Lieutenant Young stated, among other things, that the country was exceedingly healthy. As to navigating the rivers, steamers could be so constructed as to be able to go up at any time. There was no reason why communication between Lake Nyassa and the sea should not be maintained continually. Moreover, there was plenty of fuel. Steamers could be constructed so as to take to pieces, no part weighing more than half a ton. His boiler weighed more than that, but he took it over the cataracts, and nothing was lost or injured. He quite agreed with what had been said about communication by telegraph. At the northern end of Lake Nyassa they were not so very far from Lake Tanganyika, from which communication could, without much trouble, be made with the Nile, and so on to Cairo. In flood times the Zambezi would rise twenty-four feet, and run to the sea at a pretty rapid rate. There was an abundance of all kinds of game in the country, especially elephants. The natives, for the most part, caught game in pitfalls. They had only old flint-lock muskets *The way in which the slave trade was carried on was something frightful.* The Arabs would come down wanting so many slaves, and surround a village so that there should be no escape, and after capturing the men, women, and children, they would slaughter the old people on the spot. *He had seen skeletons by the thousand.* The natives wore cotton of a very coarse kind, and they much preferred our calico. Some of them were dressed in skins, but they got cloth from the Arabs. Ivory was almost as expensive as it would be in England.

"Not very long ago a woman who had made her escape from a slave gang crossed the Zambezi and came back again. She was picked up in the grass and brought to him. The opening of the Zambezi would be destructive to the slave trade, inasmuch as it would lead to the cultivation of the soil and development of commerce. Supposing that it was decided to carry a line of telegraph through Central Africa, he did not apprehend any danger about the poles being burnt or other destruction occasioned. Any amount of timber could be got for poles; in fact, it was a most magnificent country. Cape Town and its neighbourhood was the only barren part of Africa that he had seen. The distance from the lake to the sea was about 450 miles altogether, but when once the cataracts were passed there were no sandbanks or other impediments to navigation; and as to the cost of transport, he could only say that for carrying fifty to sixty pounds a distance of eighty miles he paid four yards of calico. There was no reason, however, why a road should not be made by native labour, which would much facilitate transport where navigation was impracticable."—*Cape Standard and Mail* of January 9, 1877.

We now come to the final impressions recorded by Captain Cameron of a sojourn of three years in Central Africa, both in the interior and on the coast.

"I only desire to show the present condition of the large and fertile country I have traversed, the different routes by which it may be approached, and in what manner they may be utilised, and, above all, how the utilisation of these routes may best serve to develop the vast latent resources of the country, and remove that blot on the boasted civilisation of the nineteenth century, 'the cursed slave trade.'

"Slaves, ivory, beeswax, and india-rubber are now the only articles exported from either coast, with the exception of a small and local trade from the eastern littoral in gum-copal and grain.

"Of these, ivory and slaves occupy such a prominent position, that it would be hardly worth while to mention the others, were it not that the existing trade in them proves that commerce in other articles besides slaves and ivory may be made profitable. . . .

"The whole trade of tropical Africa is at present dependent on human beings as beasts of burden, and valuable labour which may be profitably employed in cultivating the ground, or collecting products for exportation is thus lost. . . .

"The internal trade is principally carried on by slaves of merchants residing at the coast, and—as is always the case with those equally low in the scale of civilisation—they are the most cruel oppressors of all who fall into their clutches.

"Ivory is not likely to last for ever (or for long), as the main export from Africa; indeed the ruthless manner in which the elephants are destroyed and harassed has already began to show its effects. . . . Having this probable extinction of the ivory trade in view, and allowing, as all sensible people must, that legitimate commerce is the proper way to open up and civilise a country, we must see what other lucrative sources of trade may hereafter replace that in ivory.

"Fortunately we have not far to go; for the vegetable and mineral products of this marvellous land are equal in variety, value, and quantity to those of the most favoured portions of the globe. And if the inhabitants can be employed in their exploitation, vast fortunes will reward those who may be the pioneers of commerce; but the first step necessary towards this is the establishment of proper means of communication. . . .

"Already the rind of the continent has been pierced, and the Scotch missionaries on Lake Nyassa have demonstrated the feasibility of transporting a steamer past rapids, and have established a settlement on the shores of that lake. Mr. Cotterill is now engaged in tentative trade in the same direction, and I have no doubt that his efforts will be crowned with success. . . . Missionary efforts, however, will not avail to stop the slave trade, and open the country to civilisation, unless supplemented by commerce. Commercial enterprise and missionary effort, instead of acting in opposition, as is too often the case, should do their best to assist each other. . . .

"The philanthropic efforts of his Majesty the King of the Belgians, if they meet with the support they deserve, although not either of a missionary or commercial character, must also materially assist in opening up the country.

"The establishment of depots or stations on a trunk route across the continent, where the tired and weary explorer may find a resting-place and fresh stores, and men to carry on his task, cannot fail to do much towards systematising the work of discovery, instead of leaving every man to hunt for his own needle in his own bundle of hay.

"The establishment of these stations would necessitate the maintenance of regular means of communication between them, and therefore each new explorer would be able to travel direct to the one which is to serve as the base of his operations, without wasting time, money, and energy in getting into a new country. These stations may either be commanded by Europeans, or by men of character amongst the Arab merchants, who might be thoroughly relied on to do their duty in an upright and honourable manner.

"By commencing from both coasts, a chain of stations, some two hundred miles apart, might be established in a comparatively short space of time; but money is needed.

"There are many men well fitted to take charge of these expeditions, whose means do not allow them to travel on their own account, but who would volunteer in hundreds if they could see their way to aiding in the work, without endangering their scanty fortunes. . .

"Many people may say that the rights of native chiefs to govern their countries must not be interfered with. I doubt whether there is a country in Central Africa where the people would not soon welcome and rally round a settled form of government. The rule of the chiefs over their subjects is capricious and barbarous, and death or mutilation is ordered and carried out at the nod of a drunken despot.

"The negroes always seem prone to collect round any place where they may be comparatively safe from the constant raids of their enemies, and thus the settlements of both east and west coast traders frequently become *nuclei* of considerable native populations. . . .

"The question now before the civilised world is, whether the Slave Trade in Africa, *which causes, at the lowest estimate, an annual loss of over half a million lives,* is to be permitted to continue?

"Every one worthy of the name of a man will say, No!

"Let us then hope that England, which has hitherto occupied the proud position of being foremost amongst the friends of the unfortunate slave, may still hold that place.

"Let those who seek to employ money now lying idle, join together to open the trade of Africa.

"Let those interested in scientific research, come forward and support the King of the Belgians in his noble scheme for united and systematic exploration.

"Let those who desire to stamp out the traffic in slaves, put their shoulders to the wheel in earnest, and by their voice, money, and energy aid those to whom the task may be intrusted.

"Let those interested in missionary efforts, aid to their utmost those who are labouring in Africa, and send them worthy assistants, prepared to devote their lives to the task.

"It is not by talking and writing that Africa is to be regenerated, but by action. Let each one who thinks he can lend a helping hand do so. All cannot travel, or become missionaries and traders; but they can give their cordial assistance to those whose duty leads them to the as yet untrodden places of the world.

"But I would impress upon all who approach this question the necessity for not being too sanguine. Many a name must be added to the roll of those who have fallen in the cause of Africa, much patient and enduring labour must be gone through without flinching or repining, before we see Africa truly free and happy.

"I firmly believe that opening up proper lines of communication will do much to check the cursed traffic in human flesh, and that the extension of legitimate commerce will ultimately put an end to it altogether. . . .

"And with regard to education and civilisation, we must be satisfied to work gradually, and not attempt to force our European customs and manners upon a people who are at present unfitted for them. . . .

"Let us therefore work soberly and steadily, never being driven back or disheartened by any apparent failure or rebuff; but, should such be met with, search for the remedy, and then press on all the more eagerly. And so in time, with God's blessing on the work, Africa may be free and happy." *Across Africa,* vol. ii. chapter xvii.

In the midst of the difficulties and even misgivings which every undertaking of an exalted character must at the beginning inevitably have to encounter, these last words acquire a special significance. All the friends of the undertaking which the African Association proposes to itself, will keenly appreciate the manly advice of the intrepid traveller. Moreover, public opinion has vigorously seconded what the Association has begun; scarcely six months have passed since its foundation, and the future of the undertaking presents itself under the best of auguries. The Belgian Committee, formed at the close of last year, has devoted itself with energy to its duties, and it already has at its disposal very considerable resources which are receiving daily accessions.

Abroad, the enterprise has everywhere met with zealous promoters. The Royal Geographical Society of London has just set on foot, under its own auspices, a Special African Fund, to be devoted to the systematic exploration of that continent; and in stipulating for an interchange of views and information bearing on that object, with similar institutions of other countries, the Society carries into execution one of the essential elements of the programme drawn up at Brussels. There are old and generous traditions among the English people, which sanction the hope that the other interests involved will not fail to be actively protected simply because they are intrusted to other hands. If England, in adopting this peculiar mode of offering its co-operation, deviates in some respects from the International Union established by the Brussels Conference, she does not the less support its views and its object, and we may be allowed to trust that she will impose upon herself exertions all the more energetic that she has come to the determination to act alone.

In most countries the undertaking can reckon upon august and powerful patronage. The King of Sweden, and the King of Saxony, the Grand Duke Constantine of Russia, the Grand Dukes of Baden and of Weimar, the Crown Prince of Denmark, the Archduke Charles Louis of Austria, are already enrolled as honorary members of the International Association. The organisation of the Association is everywhere progressing. The Committees of Germany, of Austria, of Spain, and of the Netherlands are formed, and are about to enter without delay upon the period of action. That of France is on the eve of being regularly constituted. National Committees are also being formed on the most favourable conditions in Italy, in Switzerland, and in Portugal. The co-operation of the United States of America was secured from the commencement. In all these countries the affiliated sections are established on broad and strong bases; they adopt the programme and conform to the resolutions of the International Conference of the month of September last. It is impossible that so imposing a combination of forces, acting under the influence of one and the same feeling, should not lead, after a comparatively short space of time, to results corresponding to the extent of the effort and the grandeur of the design.

To sum up, the Association for the exploration and civilisation of Central Africa now rests on a solid foundation. Its action will proceed from two distinct centres, but will concentrate itself upon the same object and be actuated by the same principles. A genuine solidarity will protect all the enterprises whether individual or national, and will henceforth subordinate them to one common purpose. This fact, and it may be assumed to be an accomplished fact, forms the climax of the present position. If it should not succeed in absolutely preventing partial disagreements, it will at least contribute to allay them and to confine them within such limits as shall prevent them from being dangerous to the progress of science and the welfare of humanity.

www.ingramcontent.com/pod-product-compliance
Lightning Source LLC
Chambersburg PA
CBHW020918230426
43666CB00008B/1485